BANJO
on the
MOUNTAIN

Publicity photo, mid-1930s.

BANJO
on the
MOUNTAIN

Wade Mainer's First Hundred Years

Dick Spottswood
With an essay by Stephen Wade

University Press of Mississippi / Jackson

www.upress.state.ms.us

The University Press of Mississippi is a member of the
Association of American University Presses.

Library of Congress Cataloging-in-Publication Data

Spottswood, Richard K. (Richard Keith)
Banjo on the mountain : Wade Mainer's first hundred
years / Dick Spottswood, with an essay by Stephen Wade.
    p. cm. — (American made music series)
Includes index.
    ISBN 978-1-60473-577-2 (cloth : alk. paper) —
    ISBN 978-1-60473-498-0 (pbk. : alk. paper) —
ISBN 978-1-60473-499-7 (ebook) 1. Mainer, Wade, 1907–
    2. Country musicians—United States—Biography.
        3. Banjoists—United States—Biography.
            I. Wade, Stephen. II. Title.
                ML419.M213S66 2010
                782.421642092—dc22
[B]   2009054382

British Library Cataloging-in-Publication Data available

Contents

Preface

I'll never forget when I was a child going to school. I'd pass these houses and hear Mainers' Mountaineers singing those old songs they did on Bluebird records. If I heard a song that way one time, I could sing it the next time I heard it. I had a first cousin that had an old crank-up record player. I remember that he had "Maple on the Hill" by Mainer's Mountaineers, and "Take Me in the Lifeboat" and all those songs. If I was walking to school and heard them, I would always stop, which would make me late.
—CARL SAUCEMAN, Donaldsonville, Louisiana, 1973

Carl Sauceman (1922–2005) remembered hearing the Mainers' music as he grew up in rural East Tennessee. When I was small I was drawn to country music too, along with daily serial dramas, crackly transmissions from World War II European battle fronts, oracular pronouncements from evening news disseminators Gabriel Heatter and Lowell Thomas, little boy adventure shows like *The Lone Ranger*, *Jack Armstrong (The All American Boy)*, *Terry and the Pirates*, *The Adventures of Frank Merriwell*, *The Shadow*, and other things that AM radio had to offer in the 1940s. Our family radio was a prewar Philco, housed in a big wooden cabinet that claimed the corner behind my father's armchair next to the fireplace. Controls were on top, beneath a hinged lid that I could only reach by standing on a footstool. With its big loop antenna, the radio could pull in shortwave broadcasts, and I could hear WFMD in Frederick, Maryland, whose signal from forty miles away featured live and recorded country music. My mother didn't think much of my tastes, but she let me listen as long as I didn't crank up the sound.

Wade Mainer records were aired frequently enough that I came to recognize his name, along with Ernest Tubb, Roy Acuff, Elton Britt, Bob Wills, Gene Autry, Al ("Pistol Packin' Mama") Dexter, and other big-hat music heroes.

I started first grade in 1943 and didn't hear much country music until I went to high school in 1952, when I discovered the 1920s classics presented in Harry Smith's groundbreaking *Anthology of American Folk Music* collection, which introduced me to the Carter Family, G. B. Grayson, and Dock Boggs, along with old time blues, gospel, and Cajun music. The collection's timeline ended in 1930, but Smith's album notes hinted at the 1930s delights of the Monroe Brothers, Blue Sky Boys, and Wade and J. E. Mainer, found on other old discs. By then I had become a record collector, and hunted for retro music on 78 rpm discs whenever the opportunity presented itself, and when my limited financial resources would permit.

I first heard prewar Mainer records in the homes of Mike Seeger, Pete Kuykendall, Tom Paley, and Benny Cain, and original copies in various states of wear turned up in junk stores with some frequency. I gradually discovered that the brothers were almost the only ones to retain fiddle and banjo string-band sounds from earlier days on radio and records, and I learned that their Bluebird pressings of old songs like "Maple on the Hill," "Down in the Willow Garden," "Take Me in the Lifeboat," and "Train 45" were the versions that Carl Sauceman and others in the first generation of bluegrass bands grew up hearing and learning. I loved those records too, along with a few others Wade and J. E. Mainer made for King in 1946 and 1951, and kept enjoying them as I grew older.

At the time I didn't know that three Mainer Bluebird tracks had been included in the 1941 Victor Records anthology *Smoky Mountain Ballads*, assembled for folk music enthusiasts in the North, or that Wade had evolved into a folk singer in the eyes of the Lomaxes, the Roosevelts, *Life* magazine, and other culture arbiters. Lead Belly, Sonny Terry, Woody Guthrie, and Josh White were other southern performers whose folk authenticity was determined and handed to them in New York, along with new "folk songs" matching the social and political protocols of the time. Their mediated appeal to sophisticated urban audiences was comparable to that of Burl Ives, Susan Reed, Pete Seeger, and other early folk revival stars. Cousin Emmy, Muddy Waters, Son House, the Coon Creek Girls, and Wade Mainer were also recorded by Alan Lomax, but they didn't move to New York City, and their subsequent lives weren't shaped by the folk revival. Wade was probably the least known of the lot, even if his "authenticity" credentials were as good as anyone's. Though he sang for the Roosevelts in 1941 in Washington and for the BBC in 1943 in New York, his career and audience remained in the southern mountains, and he did not perform at folk music events again until the 1970s. A tantalizing postscript: Wade remembers making studio recordings with Woody Guthrie in 1943, but they have yet to be located.

Wade and Julia Mainer rediscovered their faith and grew closer to the church when Wade abandoned music and moved to Michigan for permanent work with General Motors in 1953. Few coworkers there knew he'd previously been a professional performer. Outside the church there were few occasions to make music until he retired in 1972. I still lived in Washington when the couple came to local festivals and other events. On one occasion, Wade, Julia, and their son, the late Leon Mainer, appeared at the National Folk Festival in Reston, Virginia, reuniting with 1930s colleagues Steve Ledford and Wiley and Zeke (the Morris Brothers), to recreate the classics they'd first performed forty years earlier. The Mainers appeared at the Delaware Valley Bluegrass Festival in the seventies and eighties. Figure 71 [2501376] shows Wade there with one of his many fans.

Over the years, Wade and Julia have been interviewed for newspapers, magazines, radio, television, dissertations, and history books. Unavoidably they've become used to repeating the same answers to the same questions put to them by chroniclers who bring varying degrees of familiarity with the Mainers to their task.

I became one of those chroniclers in 2006, when I annotated the booklet accompanying Gusto Records' collection of Wade's recordings on King from the 1940s to the 1960s (see discography for details). Wade then asked if I would give him, Julia, and their music a book-length treatment. When Wade Mainer asks, you don't say no. So I agreed to think about it, though it was hard to imagine creating a book-length narrative out of a career that was interrupted in Wade's musical prime by his need for steady employment and security that music could no longer provide. Economically it was clearly the right decision at the time, but it meant that the 1960s folk revival that revived the careers and underscored the historical importance of major performers like Dock Boggs, Bill Monroe, John Hurt, Doc Watson, Skip James, Son House, and the Carter Family had to make do without the Mainers.

Fortunately Wade and Julia have enjoyed many years of performing since 1972, when they were pleasantly surprised to learn that Wade's music still attracted audiences. They took it around the country and abroad, supplementing Wade's retirement income and allowing new fans to enjoy the rich string band sounds that sired and inspired bluegrass. Michigan is an active bluegrass state, and the Mainers have frequently performed for their many fans and friends there. As Wade notes, fans haven't always grasped the fine points of distinction between his music and bluegrass, but he is happy to present it under any rubric they choose.

Thanks to Stephen Wade, Bob Carlin, Penny Parsons, Gary Reid, Eddie Stubbs, Pete and Kitsy Kuykendall, Stan Werbin (Elderly Instruments, Inc.), Doug Seroff, and especially to Frank, Kelly, Randy, Polly Mainer Hofmeister, and Ralph Frederick, supportive and loving members of the Mainer Family who have helped and encouraged me in this gratifying project. Special thanks to Dr. David Evans, whose critical reading of my manuscript made it better, and to my editor Craig Gill for allowing me to join the ranks of distinguished University Press of Mississippi music authors.

BANJO
on the
MOUNTAIN

The Wade Mainer Story

Wade Mainer's long and rewarding life story has been told many times, as it deserves to be. Coming out of a rich musical environment in western North Carolina, he has taken the sounds he grew up with and shaped them according to his own creative instincts, preserving his distinctive brand of mountain music on a series of recordings stretching back seventy-five years, and appearing on music-making occasions to this day, well into the second century of his life.

Wade kept the sound of America's greatest indigenous instrument, the five-string banjo, alive during the lean years of the 1930s, when it was rejected as old-fashioned and corny by many country music fans and an emerging country music industry that sought broader, less regionalized markets. Wade's distinctive two-finger picking technique was emulated by young musicians like Ed Amos, Ralph Stanley, Wiley Birchfield, Hoke Jenkins, and others who kept the sounds of early banjo music current until the Earl Scruggs three-finger roll came to define bluegrass and dominate old-time music in the early 1950s—and even Scruggs owed something to Wade's distinctive version of "Old Ruben," recorded, released, and largely overlooked in 1941, when the United States was gearing up to join its European allies to fight in World War II.

The banjo itself was brought to the American colonies by enslaved West Africans. Early variations were called *banza, bangeon, bangelo,* and *banjar,* among other names. In the nineteenth century, the banjo was an indispensable feature of staged minstrel shows, where its distinctive sound symbolized southern plantation life. A standardized design, featuring four strings along a narrow neck and a drone fifth string, evolved in the 1830s. After the Civil War, banjos were mass-produced and became popular amateur instruments. Mail order catalogs made them available throughout the South, where they joined fiddles in informal rural dance bands.

Minstrel shows with white performers were on the wane by 1900, but banjo-playing comics survived in country life. Early country record-makers in the 1920s included Dock Walsh, George "Shortbuckle" Roark, Land Norris, and especially Uncle Dave Macon, perpetuating minstrel banjo comedy for their generation. Macon's starring role for a quarter century on the Grand Ole Opry ensured the banjo's identification with country music. Other early records featured string bands like the Carolina Tar Heels and Charlie Poole's North Carolina Ramblers, where banjos provided rhythmic support and counterpoint to a lead fiddler or, in the case of the Tar Heels, a harmonica.

With his older brother J. E. (Joseph Emmett) Mainer (1898–1971), Wade formed a string band that freed them both from cotton mill work in the Depression years and went on to dominate the airwaves in North Carolina and beyond in the 1930s. J.E. was a robust hoedown fiddler and entertainer whose music was deeply rooted in the rough-and-ready traditions of Gid Tanner's Skillet Lickers and Fiddlin' John Carson. When he was 12, J.E. followed his father W.J. (William Joseph) Mainer (1850–1947), who moved to Glendale, South Carolina, to work in a cotton mill. Later, J.E. moved on to Concord, North Carolina, to work in a larger mill, keeping his fiddle and banjo tuned for dances and frolics.

According to Wade, "My two older brothers worked in the mill and they had no child labor law then. Work was hard, and I heard my brothers tell how they were treated. Dad got word of this and confronted the people, telling them it had better not happen again. My dad was a big mountain man, and people took notice. My dad was a real good singer—real stout voice. I do a lot of his old songs. He sung that old tune that I put on a record called 'Take Me in Your Lifeboat,' and he knew a lot of those old, old songs."

Wade Eckhart Mainer (the spelling of his middle name is uncertain) was born on April 21, 1907, as he recalls, "in a three- or four-room log house, several miles from Asheville, with no electric, no water in the house, no bath in the house. We had an outside toilet, a

W.J. and Polly Mainer family photo, c. 1912. L to R: Gertrude, Eva, Willis, W.J., Essie, Wade, Finley, Polly, J.E., James.

galvanized tin tub to bathe in, and read the Bible at night by the old oil lamp. Mom and Dad was very religious and taught us to fear God and treat people right.

"Transportation was either to walk, thumb a ride in a buggy or wagon . . . of course there was a mule or a horse, if a person had one. It was kind of rough back in the days that I grew up. We were raised poor people back in the mountains."

When W.J. had saved enough from his job at the mill, he bought a small mountain farm in Reems Creek, near Weaverville in Buncombe County, western North Carolina, where Wade remembers that "my two brothers and sister and myself had to walk over Hamburg Mountain and down the other side to a two-room school at Dooley Springs, on Little Flat Creek. The second school I attended was Chestnut Grove, which was about the same distance. There was no school in the winter and, having to help Dad on the farm, I did not get but very little education."

Sometimes Wade and his brothers would hunt squirrels and rabbits, cleaning and dressing them so that his parents could take them to Asheville in their horse cart on Saturdays. To augment the family income, he remembers that his mother, Polly Rebecca Mainer (1870–1944), "would churn milk, make butter, gather up eggs, dress out chickens . . . Mom and Dad would put this in the wagon, would leave early in the morning to go to Asheville, about eight or nine miles from where we lived. They would walk the street peddling until they sold what they'd brought. Then they would buy flour, sugar, coffee, salt, or whatever they needed."

Every fall, W.J. would dig a big hole in the ground, cover the bottom with straw, and gather anything that would keep through the winter, laying them on the straw bed and covering them with more straw and dirt. When Polly needed vegetables for dinner, she would dig out what she needed and re-cover the rest.

When Wade was in his teens, his older sister Essie married a sawmill operator named Roscoe Banks. "I worked at my brother-in-law's sawmill for around a week. He was a good left-handed fiddler and his brother Will was a banjo picker. On Saturday nights there was generally a square dance in the neighborhood. I'd go and watch and, when they would lay their music down, why I'd pick up the banjo and I'd start trying to play it." It was a small if solid beginning, and Roscoe soon gave Wade a homemade banjo of his own.

"I left home when I was eighteen or nineteen and went to Marion to stay with my sister, Eva Coates, and work on construction for a while. I didn't stay long, went back home for a while and went back to Marion to stay with my brother James and work at a cotton mill in East Marion. Later on I went to Concord, where J.E. lived. He was married and working at a cotton mill, playing fiddle on the side. I got a job in the mill, and J.E. and I would play music in our spare time, for parties, corn shuckings, lassy pullings [molasses making], bean stringings, and fiddlers' conventions."

Focusing on entertainment, Wade and J.E. rarely played for dances, although fiddle tunes later became an integral part of their radio and stage shows. Forming a band with the guitar-picking brothers Howard and Lester Lay in 1932, they initially worked on radio at WSOC in Gastonia, alternating music with mill work.

Their career took off in 1934 when a banjo-playing entertainer, Fisher Hendley, encouraged them to audition for promoter J.W.

Fincher, whose Crazy Water Crystals was an aggressively marketed laxative compound. Fincher sponsored other popular North Carolina radio performers, including the Monroe Brothers, Dixon Brothers, and Blue Sky Boys. Across the South, the Crazy Water radio talent roster included Roy Acuff in Knoxville and Bob Wills in Tulsa. Even Hank Snow was sponsored by Crazy Water Crystals on mid-1930s broadcasts from Halifax, Nova Scotia. Dubbing them the Crazy Mountaineers, Fincher welcomed the Mainers into the fold, allowing them to become full-time professionals and say goodbye once and for all to the cotton mill.

When their WBT (Charlotte, North Carolina) engagement began in 1934, the Mountaineers consisted of Wade and J.E. with guitarists Claude Edward "Zeke" Morris (1916–1999) and Daddy John Love, who was replaced by Boyden Carpenter ("The Hillbilly Kid") in 1935. By then Wade had become a smooth, radio-friendly singer and distinctive banjo player. WBT's strong signal could be heard throughout much of western North Carolina, where radio exposure, including daily live shows and the Crazy Barn Dance on Saturday nights, provided the Mainers with all the work they could handle. Life was not easy for the musicians, even after they became well known. Early morning radio appearances and tiring drives over rough country roads to shows in remotely located grange halls and schoolhouses made for a better life than the Mainers had known as mill workers, but was an exhausting schedule just the same. Admission prices to their shows were twenty-five to fifty cents, and large, enthusiastic audiences turned music-making into a viable livelihood for them.

In 1935, after working at WBT and briefly at WWL in New Orleans, the Mountaineers moved to WPTF in Raleigh, where J.E. and Wade remained until they good-naturedly parted company in 1937. By then, J.E. had grown accustomed to the security of working for J.W. Fincher and Crazy Water Crystals, while Wade and Zeke Morris preferred to part from Fincher and explore other opportunities.

Wade's sister Essie and her husband Roscoe Banks had two talented sons, Robert and Maurice, who could sing and play guitar and mandolin. When Wade asked permission to take their children on the road, the answer was affirmative, and the boys were dubbed "Buck and Buddy, the Little Smilin' Rangers." With Zeke Morris and Steve Ledford, they moved to High Point, started a radio program, and featured Buck and Buddy on an August 1937 record session.

The Smilin' Rangers arrangement ended with the start of the fall school term. On November 28, 1937, Wade married Julia Mae Brown, a talented singer, guitarist, and radio performer whom he had known since 1935. She willingly shared business chores as Wade assembled a new band . By 1938 they were on WBIG in Greensboro as Wade Mainer and Sons of the Mountaineers. Wade: "I changed Julia's name from Hillbilly Lillie to Princess. She did the bookwork and sold tickets on our appearances." And she sang, without label credit, on the band's Blue-bird record of Cliff Carlisle's song "When Romance Calls."

The Sons of the Mountaineers included bandleader Roy Hall's younger brother Jay Hugh, and an immensely talented lead singer and guitarist named Clyde Moody. Jay Hugh and Clyde had already per-formed as a Callahan Brothers–styled duet before signing with Wade, and several of his 1938 records feature them.

Work in Greensboro was not plentiful, and Wade welcomed an invitation from announcer/promoter Byron Parker to bring the Sons to WIS in Columbia, South Carolina, even though J.E. Mainer's band (with Leonard Stokes, George Morris, and Snuffy Jenkins) was already there when Wade arrived with Moody, Ledford, and Hall. They worked for around a month until Parker learned that Wade was booking shows for his band without giving him a percentage. Only then did Parker decide that two Mainer bands on WIS was one too many, so Wade and the Sons of the Mountaineers left for WSPA in Spartanburg, South Carolina.

J.E. was having drinking problems at the time and parted with his own band, which remained at WIS, hired fiddler Homer "Pappy" Sher-rill, and renamed itself Byron Parker and his Mountaineers. J.E. and Wade reunited briefly, and J.E. even recorded with Moody and Hall. But his drinking persisted, and there were problems with J.E. and Steve Ledford blending their two fiddles, so J.E. left the Sons of the Mountaineers and wound up in Texas with Buck and Buddy, perform-ing as a trio on border radio in 1941. Wade Mainer and Sons of the Mountaineers returned to Raleigh and WPTF, working there for most of 1939 until Moody, Hall, and Ledford departed to become the Happy-Go-Lucky Boys back at WSPA.

Wade built a handsome seven-room brick house on several acres in Stony Knob near Weaverville, ten miles north of Asheville, where he and Julia would begin their family.

Their first child was named after Julia's father. Wade recalls: "Our oldest son Frank was born in March 1939. When he began crawling and pulling up to chairs, Julia decided one day to take him and go to see us broadcast—WPTF wasn't too far from where we were living. She set Frank on the floor and, not long after that, the Mountaineers went off the air. Everyone scrambled around to find out what went wrong, and there was Frank, near a plug that was pulled out of the wall. One of the men saw this and, with a few laughs, the Sons of the Mountaineers were back on the air."

Lest it seem as though Wade and the Mountaineers had a particularly rocky career, it is useful to note that their migration from one radio market to another reflected the demanding occupational realities of southeastern rural entertainment in the 1930s. Money was scarce as the region recovered from the Depression, and performers could remain in one area only as long as their broadcasts persuaded listeners to attend live events. After a while any given area would be "played out" and audiences would fail to attend repeat appearances. Performers would then relocate to a new area where their appeal would be fresh for a while.

While employed at the Library of Congress in the 1930s, folklorist Alan Lomax became aware of Wade Mainer and other southern, tradition-based entertainers as he acquired collections of Paramount, Vocalion, and Bluebird 78 rpm records for the Library. In 1941 Lomax arranged for a prestigious invitation from Librarian of Congress Archibald MacLeish in Washington, requesting that Wade, fiddler Tiny Dodson, and guitarist Jack Shelton perform for the Roosevelts and guests at a private "folk music" event at the White House on the evening of February 17. Burl Ives, Josh White, and the Golden Gate Quartet were also featured.

Interviewed for a 1981 re-creation of the occasion, Wade gave the Smithsonian Institution's Ralph Rinzler a firsthand account of his experience:

On February 10, 1941, I received a letter from Mr. Alan Lomax asking me to appear at the concert at the White House for the

President. And that's Franklin Delano Roosevelt and, of course, I was very excited. I was getting ready to go on the air at that time; I was on the Farm Hour in Asheville, WWNC, in North Carolina, and I got so excited that I like not to have got over my program. But anyway we accepted the invitation. I took Tiny Dodson and Jack Shelton and we loaded up the old car. That was in February, and we headed out for Washington. When we got in there it was a little bit chilly.

So we went on and entered the White House, got all set up and fixed up and everything, and got ourselves together. I forget what day it was that we appeared out in the Blue Room at the White House to entertain Mr. Roosevelt and Mrs. Roosevelt and [Secretary of the Navy] Frank Knox. At that time they had several hundred people there of the big executives. So we played and they seemed to like our program pretty well.

After it was over, I went in and met the President and shook hands with him. I thought he had one of the friendliest, most warm handshakes that I ever had anybody to shake hands with. And he was very nice and talked to me about North Carolina. He asked how the people were doing and how they were getting along. I told him everybody seemed to be getting along real good since he got to be President and brought us out of the Depression. He asked me then what about the tobacco crops and what about your cotton crops and so on and so forth. So I talked a little bit to him about that. I don't know how he got a hold of me being a farmer or anything, unless someone told him I was on the Farm Hour on WWNC doing an hour's program a day for the farmers. Maybe that's where he picked up that I was a farmer.

Anyway, after we had a good long talk and it seemed like everything worked out real good, they had us come in for ice cream and cake and cookies and so on. All those goodies and everything, you know. Mrs. Roosevelt, she was there, and I got me a bowl of ice cream and was standing there by one of those bat-wing doors: when you push one open, you know, why it would fly back and forth.

LIBRARY OF CONGRESS

WASHINGTON

February 10, 1941

Dear Mr. Mainer:

    On the evening of February 17, Mrs. Roosevelt is going to give a folk song party at the White House and she has asked me to help her arrange the program. I should like for you, Tiny Dodson and Jack Shelton to appear as Wade Mainer and His Mountainers on the program. I would like to have the entire band but that is impractical for this particular evening. Your travel, to and from Washington by bus will be paid, plus $5.00 a day for living expenses. If you can come, I should like to have you meet me at the Library of Congress, west basement door, in the early afternoon on Sunday the 16th. We will rehearse on Sunday and again on Monday for the program on Monday night. I should like your singing and playing to be as "old timey" as possible and possibly you'll do "the Willow Garden", " the Arkansas Treveller" with fiddle, " the Old Hen Cackle" "John Hardy", "Ground Hog" and numbers of this kind.

    Later on you may expect a formal invitation from the White House, but in the meantime, let me know as soon as possible whether you and the other two can come. I certainly look forward to meeting you and working with you.

          Sincerely yours,

          Alan Lomax

          Alan Lomax
          Assistant in Charge
          Archive of American Folk Song
          Library of Congress

1941 Alan Lomax letter.

LIBRARY OF CONGRESS

CE OF THE LIBRARIAN   WASHINGTON

February 14, 1941

Dear Mr. Mainer:

    I have been asked by Mrs. Roosevelt to arrange an evening of folk music at the White House on Monday evening, February 17 at 9 P. M. I take great pleasure in inviting you and the two other members of your group to take part. We all look forward with the keenest anticipation to the hearing of the folk songs which you present so movingly.

    In accordance with White House usage, no advance publicity may be given out in regard to the concert. The White House will doubtless issue an account of the evening afterwards.

    Looking forward to seeing you and your fellow performers on Monday evening, I am,

          Cordially yours,

          Archibald MacLeish

          Archibald MacLeish
          The Librarian of Congress

Mr. Wade Mainer & His Mountaineers
In Care of Radio Station WWNC
Asheville
North Carolina

1941 Archibald MacLeish letter.

Station WWNC, 570 kilocycles, 1000 watts, is owned and operated by The Asheville Citizen-Times Company, Asheville, North Carolina, and affiliated with CBS. Direct correspondence about the Western North Carolina Farm Hour and other selling shows is invited.

You are **NOT** *invited to*

AN EVENING OF AMERICAN FOLKLORE

ARRANGED BY ALAN LOMAX
ARCHIVE OF AMERICAN FOLK SONG,
LIBRARY OF CONGRESS

at

The White House

February Seventeenth

1 9 4 1

1941 WWNC "invitation."

WADE When I went to the White House I took Tiny Dodson and Jack Shelton.

At that time we were wearing bib overalls, red bandanas. I've still got those overalls hanging out in the garage. I went and played for the president with those overalls on. He shook my hand and said to sit down in a chair there. He talked with me a little while; the first or second thing he said was, "What do the people up there in NC think of me being their president?" And I said, "Mr. Roosevelt," I said, "They like you!" He grinned, you know, and we talked about ten or fifteen minutes."

I helped elect the governor of North Carolina in them overalls too. That was Kerr Scott; I went out and campaigned with him in 1948 and he got elected. [See page 76.]

Mr. Lomax, you can be certain, has gathered the top talent from the nation. Among those performing will be the

SONS OF THE MOUNTAINEERS

from W W N C's

WESTERN NORTH CAROLINA FARM HOUR

The Western North Carolina Farm Hour, staged by Mardi Liles, WWNC's farmer par excellence, is of, for, and by the farmers of our sixteen county state within a state. Available in fifteen minute periods to those who would dominate this region, WWNC's Western North Carolina Farm Hour represents one of the greatest sales mediums for farm products.

So I was standing right there and Mrs. Roosevelt went out for something. And when she came back, she pushed the door open and it hit me and knocked the bowl of ice cream out of my hand and knocked it on her. So of course, me being an old country boy and I ain't never been in the big city much before and everything. So I run my hand down in my pocket and pulled out a big old red bandana handkerchief, I was going to wipe the ice cream off of her. She said, "No, you just forget about that." She disappeared for a few minutes and directly she came back, she had on a different dress and everything. The concert went on and it was a very lovely evening that we had down there with them at the White

WWNC, 1941. Standing, L to R: Curly Shelton, Tiny Dodson, Howard Dixon. Kneeling L to R: Jack Shelton, Wade Mainer.

House. (From the Smithsonian Museum program, *Folk Music in the Roosevelt White House: An Evening of Song, Recollections and Dance,* Sunday, January 31, 1982.)

Shortly after the Sons of the Mountaineers' command appearance, Alan Lomax traveled to Asheville to record a simulated Farm Hour broadcast at WWNC with Wade's complete band, including Howard Dixon (of the Dixon Brothers) and staff announcer Marty Lyles. Alan also made recordings of W.J. Mainer's unaccompanied singing before returning to Washington. In the summer of 1941, his father, folklorist John A. Lomax, included three 1936–37 Mainer tracks in an influential five-disc Victor album called *Smoky Mountain Ballads,* comprised of "folk songs" reissued from the Victor and Bluebird country catalogs and marketed to a northern cosmopolitan audience whose idea of folk music was then defined by sophisticated entertainers like Burl Ives, Susan Reed, and Richard Dyer-Bennett. The Carter Family, Dixon Brothers, Monroe Brothers, Arthur Smith, Gid Tanner, and Uncle Dave Macon were represented on the Victor set too, and thus introduced to many northern folk song enthusiasts for the first time.

In September 1941, Wade did a final session for RCA in Atlanta after a two-year absence from the recording studio. This was the date that produced the memorable "Old Ruben," Wade's version of a hobo song learned from his brother-in-law and early mentor Roscoe Banks. Though the tune, also known as "Train 45" and "Nine Hundred Miles," was a familiar standard, Wade's record was the first to feature a banjo. Later, China Poplin, Fred Cockerham, Cousin Emmy, Dock Boggs, and other pre-bluegrass pickers recorded it that way. Earl Scruggs has made an earlier claim, recalling that "the year was 1934 and I was ten years old . . . I was sitting there in the room picking 'Reuben' in D tuning,"[1] when he worked out a three-finger roll that became the cornerstone of bluegrass.

In the fall of 1941, with new records on the market and unprecedented attention from national celebrities, Wade's career should have been on a roll. Instead, while he was in Knoxville at WNOX in November, the station management forced him to refuse an offer to appear on the Grand Ole Opry. Following that disappointment, *Life* magazine dispatched photographer Eric Schaal to take pictures for a feature on Wade and J.E., the Carter Family, and Bascom Lamar Lunsford. The planned article should have been a celebration of traditional country music. Instead, it was canceled when Pearl Harbor was bombed on December 7, 1941.

The war years became lean ones. Wade returned from Knoxville to North Carolina to rejoin his growing family, which now included a new son, Kelly. The Mainers purchased some property from Julia's father in Mocksville, where Wade registered for the draft and waited for the call that never came. Though he was spared military service, wartime rationing of tires, gasoline, and other essentials made travel difficult, and performance opportunities became infrequent. Fortunately the farm was there for times when music work was scarce. The Mainers still owned the house Wade had built in Weaverville, and the family alternated between both places in the 1940s.

Wade was working in the Atlanta area when Julia gave birth to twins Leon and Polly on August 16, 1944. Around that time, Alan Lomax invited Wade and J.E. to assemble a band and travel to New York to perform in a morale-boosting wartime broadcast for the BBC network in England. *The Old Chisholm Trail* was produced on or around September 11 at the BBC studio at 630 5th Avenue, with a cast that also starred Woody Guthrie, Burl Ives, Cisco Houston, Sonny Terry, and the Coon Creek Girls. The Mainer outfit included teenage cousins Red Rector and Fred Smith, playing their first professional music job. Red later recalled singing "Bury Me Not on the Lone Prairie" in a trio with Fred and Wade.

Wade Mainer made a group of King Records in the autumn of 1946, five years after his last RCA session in 1941. King had been gradually launched after Cincinnati record retailer Syd Nathan issued a couple of experimental releases in 1943; the label became a serious player in the growing country music industry after he formed a corporation in August 1944. Nathan's move was well timed; a 1942–43 strike by the American Federation of Musicians against major labels had given King (and other small manufacturers who agreed to AFM terms) temporary respite from big-label competition and a chance to place their regional music into wider distribution. Even though wartime

Cast of *The Old Chisholm Trail* BBC broadcast, New York City, September 11, 1944. L to R: Wade, Red Rector, J.E., Fred Smith, Cisco Houston, Rosie Ledford, Woody Guthrie, Lee Hays, Sonny Terry, Susie Ledford, Burl Ives, Lily May Ledford. Used with permission of the Woody Guthrie Archives.

rationing made raw materials scarce, King became a force to contend with in the burgeoning country and rhythm and blues arenas. The label turned regional country artists into major acts, and Wade joined Grandpa Jones, the Delmore Brothers, Clyde Moody, Cowboy Copas, Moon Mullican, Wayne Raney, the Bailes Brothers, and Hawkshaw Hawkins, all household names in the postwar country music environment.

J.E. Mainer had already made some memorable titles for King in June 1946, featuring his old-time singing, fiddling, and occasional banjo playing. For his own King debut several months later (precise recording dates have not survived), Wade produced a group of somber

Recording *The Old Chisholm Trail* at the BBC studios, New York City, September 11, 1944. L to R: Eugene (Red) Rector, Woody Guthrie, Fred Smith, J.E. Mainer, Cisco Houston, Wade Mainer. Used with permission of the Woody Guthrie Archives.

WADE I had to give J.E. a job. I said to him, "They asked for you; I'm going to take you to New York. Are you going to behave yourself?" He said, "I'll get in there and lay it on 'em!" We did the show and he went to the manager, told him, "I gotta have more money." He was in there sitting and drinking with the big folks. They passed it by me and I said no, I'm not drinking that stuff.

titles, focused on American families still coming to terms with war losses: "Awaiting the Return of My Boy," "Searching for a Soldier's Grave," "Mother's Prayers Have Followed Me," songs that told of dead and wounded veterans, validating and reinforcing the feelings of victims and their families.

Shortly before Wade's session, he heard from Johnnie Bailes of the Bailes Brothers, who had recently produced a marathon session of twenty-four titles for King. In a letter to Wade, Johnnie thanked him for preparing to cover "Dust on the Bible," an as yet unreleased song the Bailes had recorded for Columbia in February 1945. Wade and the group learned it and the Bailes' "Soldier's Grave" (usually "Searching for a Soldier's Grave") on the spot, calling in King Records' house

3530 MERMAID AVENUE, Brooklyn, 24., New York., Sept. 17th, 1944   Pa

Howdy, Wade, J.E., Smitty & Red:

    BBC just sent me some pictures that they took on the night that
you guys were here. I think they are mighty fine. At least it is a
good picture of a mountaineer band with no silly rube costumes on. I
never did like to see hillbilly people dressed up like a bunch of clowns
but lots of radio people still think of us as that way, and want to take
damn fool pictures of us. You four boys look awful good and natural in
these pictures. Wade, you've got your eyes closed like you were howling
up at the moon, (wishing for a good car and lots of gas to go touring
with) -- your banjo is so plain I can even count the strings, and see the
thumb pick jumping around on your thumb -- I can hear that loping old
banjo, too, just as plain as daylight.
    J.E., you've got a look on your face like you really loved that
fiddle, and every hair in that bow, even the smell of that rosum flying
up off those strings; you handle that neck of your fiddle like it was
something you really loved. I can see a dreamy look in your eyes that
seems like you're drifting back down across all of the days of your life
while you're knocking off that tune. No doubt about it, J.E., a man has
got to have a lot of faith in the human race to play the kind of music you
play and play it as good as you do. There's an eight wheeler drive in
all the soundsypuu get, and your memories, I suppose, run just about the
same.
    SMITTY, you're holding that big Martin box up at an angle like it was
a tommy gun poking up out of a shell hole. You're not looking at the
guitar, but right straight on out ahead of you, and into that camera.
Your belt buckle is shining like the front end of a late model car. You
hold your teeth tight together like a fast horse jerking at the bits. I
don't know what you're thinking about, probably some of the jillion and
one other good tunes that run through your mind. Probably about the
flash of that camera. (It's like having a big sized hand grenade explode
right close to you).
    AND RED, the way you hold your mouth sideways while you tickle that
mandolin, is really something. You look like a man that really believes
in something big. You've got the looks of a square jawed preacher about
your face. You seem to be trying to swallow something about the size of
a jumping frog, but you're not nervous nor not scared. You're liking
this whole business. You like these radio studios, the big ones and the
little ones. You feel at home here, and you feel like you're doing your
part of the world's labors. You know that the kind of music that you make
is in the hearts of all of us, and you know that your sounds and songs are
a part of the country that you know. You know that there is a hell of a
big fight going on all around you, and you hope your work is helping the
best people to win out. You hold that mandolin like your first born baby.
(That mandolin has really got a good deep booming tone to it when somebody
like you gets ahold of it and beats it out. I just want to tell you how
much I liked those fast railroad bluees (and such likes) peices as you
played while you were here.
    ALL FOUR OF YOU have really got something on the ball. I thought this
a long time ago when I first heard your records in the Library of Congress
in Washington. I heard you do John Henry and several others, Train 45.,
and lots of others. Of course you've got a different bunch nowdays, but
I like your set up, now, even better than then.
    I like J.E.'s fiddling now better than then. He said while he was
here that he fiddled better back in them days than he does now, that it
was 'smoother' then. You mustn't let this idea run away with you. If
you do, you'll sort of begin to get sloppy and it will become a fact.
Truth is, you got to remember that your music don't sound to other people
like it does to you. And the fact is, that there are millions of us that
like fiddle music to be just a tiny bit rough and rowdy, it sounds like
more spirit is in it, sometimes. (I hate a slicked up fiddle band. It
sounds sissy and thin to me.) You're actually bound to be fiddling better

Woody Guthrie letter, 16 September 1944. Note that
Woody dated his letter a day after the postmark on
the envelope (see page 20). Used with permission of
the Woody Guthrie Archives.

now than in the days gone by, because whatever you are today, tomorrow you surely can't be any worse, nor any less. You're bound to
be better. I listen to my own records of a few years ago and I fall
into the rut and get to worrying because I sound 'younger' or 'smoother'
or better in those days than now. But when ⊥ ask other people, they
all laugh at me and say I'm a hell of a lot better now than I ever was
in the days gone by. And you're not a bunch of old men, so it can't be
your old age slipping up on you. You're all just in the prime of your
life. You do so well for a group that you have nothing nor nobody in
the world to be afraid of. You've got to just keep your faith in your
own self and in all of your people, and keep right on believing that
you are helping us to win and keep our better world. There is nothing,
no force, no power, no explosive, no ammunition, no printed word that
is as strong a weapon as music and songs in this war. Music is one of
the most powerful weapons that is winning the common working people a
job, an income, a home, and all of the better things that we are all fight-
ing to win. (You already know this. I'm sort of a fool for trying to
act like I'm telling you).

    A musician with an instrument (singing songs) does our enemy just
as much damage, (and maybe a damn sight more) than any soldier with a
flamethrower, a grenade, or a gun. Because it is spirit that wins any
war. It's not piles of ammunition, nor stacks of bombs, nor shiploads
of war stuff. It's that old spirit that you hear ring out of those
very fiddles, banjos, mandolins, and guitars that you boys play so good.
If a Millionaire playboy or gal deserves a couple of limousines to zip
across the country in, (doing nothing), then Lord knows that men like
you rightfully deserve to tour the whole nation in an automobile as
big and long as the new morning train. And the day will come, you mark
my word, when you will feel the four winds kiss your cheeks as you ease
out across the country to bring some more of this spirit to the people.
(They say that gasoline is hard to get because our kind of work is a
'luxury'-- ha-- ha --ha. Yet, millions of gallons of it are sucked down
into the damned old carburetors of racketeers, gangsters, black market
whores and pimps every month!! These people do every earthly thing they
can do to kill and to drown and to choke the real spirit of our people,
by simply stealing this gasoline that should be going into the tanks of
our planes, tractors, and trucks to win this war against racketeers! If
they can drive around right under our noses without getting caught, then
surely they aren't being hunted very hard. I think I'll have to set down
and make up about ten good big long songs about this goddamned black
market. I really get riled up when I get to thinking about it!!)

    We had a big storm here last night and I had to walk all the way from
Coney Island up to the house. The Norton Point (Toonerville) Trolley got
flooded out and I waded water about knee deep all the way. I bucked a
wind that must of been blowing at least 80 miles an hour. It really tore
down a lot of trees and sign boards, drive ways, bridges, walls, roofs,
and knocked out a lot of plate glass windows. I guess you read all about
it, or heard about it. You ought to be glad that you left out of here
before the hurricane hit. It caused the ocean tide to come up so high
that we couldn't tell where our rainwater quit and the ocean set in.

    Cathy Ann still hollers for your Mukick. She really got a big kick
out of the playing that you done here. She's asleep now and dreaming
about dancing or something. Marjorie just spilt ice cream all over her
clean pajamas, se I've got to quit and try to get things in hand.

    I just want to say once again that I wish you boys the very best of
luck, good fortune, health, wealth and success. I hope that you get on
the world's biggest network and get heard by every human being on the
face of the earth every day. Now, ain't that about as big a wish as I
could wish for you? I'll be right there with my ear cocked up to that
speaker like an old hound dog listening. Take it easy but take it.

CATHY   MARJORIE   WOODY GUTHRIE
                            Woody Guthrie

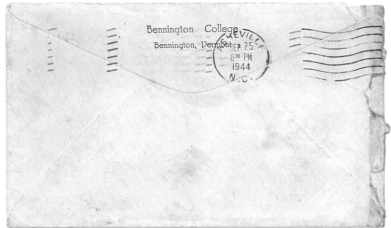

mandolinist Jethro Burns (of Homer and Jethro) to fill in for Arville Freeman, who couldn't master the songs' introductions.

Parenthetically, Johnnie's disingenuous claim "that we hardly have time for anything but work" failed to report that the Bailes Brothers had been fired from the Opry for well-publicized sexual indiscretions on Johnnie's part only a week earlier. Their original version of "Dust on the Bible" was released the same week that Johnnie wrote to Wade, and both versions sold well in the early months of 1947.

Unfortunately, Wade made no further records for another four years, and he found himself spending the immediate postwar years working on the farm as often as the stage.

GRAND OLE OPRY
NASHVILLE, TENNESSEE

Nov. 1st, 1946

Wade Mainer
  ιverville, N.C.

Dear Wade:

Sorry to be so long in answering your letter but we have been so
busy here lately that we hardly have time for anything but work.

We certainly do appreciate you recording our number and I'm sure
you did a good job and that it will sell.

Mr. Miller asked me who I'd rather have record it and we asked if
you could do it, so he said he would see you about it.

We have a lot of other numbers that are your style and if you want
to use them or record them don't hesitate to ask.

I am sending you two of our songbooks just in case you don't already
have them. Am sending our #1 and #2 folios. I hope you will be able
to use some of the songs and if you have any you would like for us
to use send them to us and we'll give them a whirl.

Here's hoping you the best of luck and we are both looking forward
to meeting you in person.

With best wishes

Johnnie Bailes
Johnnie Bailes
Bailes Brothers

RADIO, STAGE AND RECORDING ARTISTS

Wade briefly formed a band with two promising teenagers, Jim and Jesse McReynolds, when he returned to WBBO in Forest City around 1950. The outfit didn't last long and no known recordings of them survive.

After a four-and-a-half-year lapse, King summoned Wade to Charlotte to make new records on March 17, 1951, and lead a session that excluded his banjo from several titles. It was an unfortunate decision in light of the new prominence of the five-string banjo in the hands of Earl Scruggs and others.

Another 1951 session took place in King's Cincinnati studios on November 19, when Wade was joined by Troy Brammer's vigorous bluegrass band. Wade confirms that Brammer played banjo on several tracks, and band member Marion Hall sang lead vocal in Wade's place on two songs. Except for a pair of titles produced for the small Blue Ridge label in 1952, these would be the last Wade Mainer records for a full decade.

Farming and music had both become precarious livelihoods, and neither showed signs of improvement in the early 1950s. When Wade received an invitation from two traveling evangelists to join forces for a northern tour, he accepted, packed his guitar, and went to Michigan to play for a series of prayer meetings and revivals. After undergoing a spiritual conversion, Wade decided that he liked the area and would like to stay. He applied successfully for work at the General Motors auto assembly plant in Flint, where he was first hired as a polisher, then as a parts assembler, and finally as an oiler in the machine shop, tending the big machines that supported the assembly line.

Wade abandoned music, settling down to be a full-time father, husband, and breadwinner for a growing family. His and Julia's firm Christian convictions persuaded him to give up music entirely until he encountered Molly O'Day and her husband Rev. Lynn Davis when they played a revival meeting in Flint. The couple had undergone their own spiritual conversions and, for a while, abstained from performing either secular music or at secular gatherings. Molly said to Wade that the Lord had once told her that she had played long enough for the devil, and that it was now time to play for Him. Accepting her rationale, Wade allowed himself to perform sacred music and folk songs at local informal gatherings, though not often and not right away.

In 1961, King Records' Syd Nathan approached the Mainers and persuaded them to return to the company's Cincinnati studios one more time. Wade's voice never sounded better, and his banjo enjoyed a bluegrass-inspired prominence he had rarely achieved on records before. Owen Bloodworth, who lived in Flint and worked for the United Auto Workers, joined on several folk songs, singing a vigorous tenor to Wade's lead. Julia Mainer contributed "My Soldier Boy" and sang on the outstanding collection *Soulful Sacred Songs* (King 769).

Though Molly O'Day encouraged Wade to dust off his banjo and dedicate his music to the service of the Lord, his reluctance to perform continued. Except for the 1961 King date, Wade claims to have left his banjo under the bed and kept his music a closely guarded secret until he retired from General Motors in 1972. Fortunately, years of auto work diminished neither his skills nor his repertory of old songs. Soon he and Julia were enjoying a post-retirement career, performing and making records again under the encouragement of a young Brighton, Michigan, pharmacist, John Morris, who was beginning to publish records of old-time music and wanted Wade and Julia to be an important part of his growing Old Homestead catalog.

The records were well received, and they let the music world know that a still youthful sixty-five-year-old Wade Mainer was picking up his music career where he'd left off, and making room for his talented wife in the bargain. With their children grown, her domestic duties diminished, letting her join Wade and display her own long-submerged music skills. The pair were soon in demand at country music shows, college campuses, folk festivals, overseas tours, and other events. On some occasions they were joined by old colleagues like Zeke Morris or Steve Ledford. On others, sons Leon or Randall would perform alongside their parents. In 1987 Wade received the National Heritage Fellowship Award from the National Endowment for the Arts. It came with a letter of recognition from President Ronald Reagan, who wrote, "Your unique talents and achievements are a source of pride and enrichment for our Nation . . . your dedication to developing and sharing your God-given talents is a shining example of the spirit that has made America great."

Around 1:00 AM one autumn morning in 1997, Julia Mainer awoke from a sound sleep during a thunderstorm when she heard unfamiliar crackling noises. Lightning had struck an electric utility box on the Mainers' house, starting a fire that spread rapidly. Julia and Wade dressed quickly, putting their instruments and what few possessions they could save into their RV in the driveway. Most photos and documents in this book were among the things they rescued, but almost everything else was destroyed. The RV became their home for a while and they spent part of the winter with their son Randall a few miles

"THAT TWO-FINGER

WADE I had a hard time learning the banjo. I started out doing that drop thumb, clawhammer. I stayed with my sister Essie and her husband Roscoe Banks for a good long while. I worked with Roscoe in a sawmill and I guess that's where I kind of fell in love with music. Back when I was growing up there weren't too many musicians. There might have been a few old fiddlers around here and there, but there wasn't many banjos. So I took the notion that I would like the banjo. I'd slip around and pick one up when I'd get a chance.

I used to go with my brother-in-law Roscoe, who played the fiddle. They'd go and play for a square dance all night and, when they'd lay their instruments down, I'd go over and pick the banjo up. I learned on a homemade banjo. I don't know how old I was, eight, ten years old, somewhere along in there. I got to pickin' the banjo in a different style, two-finger style. I must have started in clawhammer because later on I wanted to change my style of playing, and I went to trying to pick the music out with two fingers. A lot of banjo players told me they couldn't keep good time with two fingers. They tried to learn my style and they come to me and said they couldn't keep good time like I did with the fiddle. I got the sound of three strings on my banjo, D, C, and G. I kept monkeyin' with them and, first thing you know, I felt kind of a tune that went in my head.

I had to learn myself, there was no one to teach me. The style I play in, that two-finger style banjo, I'd wrap my thumb over my forefinger and pick with my forefinger, with my thumb picking up the tone to the song in the low tuning. I really learned to play the banjo like that. I got smoother and smoother with it the longer I played.

I had good timing and J.E. had good timing with his fiddle. I did three-finger picking for awhile; I learned a three-finger wrap-around style from Walt Davis. I liked that sound but I didn't care for it too much when I couldn't keep good time. When I played with J.E. he said, "Wade, I wish you wouldn't do that; you throw me all out of time with my fiddle." He was right; when I went back to two-finger style, that's when we went over. People liked my way of playing the banjo. I wasn't doing any of that high-pitched bluegrass stuff. I stuck more or less down to the old country style; I never did change too much in my music although I had to lead out with my old banjo after awhile. That's where they got to telling me I had the bluegrass sound. I explained that I wasn't bluegrass—I played two-finger, but I hit some licks that sounded like bluegrass.

Old-time string bands normally kept banjos in the background, and Wade's playing is less prominent on most of his 1935–1951 records than later on. He played brief solos on "Always Been a Rambler" and "Short Life and It's Trouble" in 1937, but "Old Ruben" (1941) is the first where he "led out" and featured the banjo. It was an important recording, and Earl Scruggs's 1960 "Reuben" is a descendant. When Earl revitalized banjo

STYLE BANJO"

music after World War II, Wade occasionally brought his instrument forward in his ensembles, though a November 1951 King Records session instead featured Troy Brammer, who mixed Mainer and bluegrass elements in his banjo playing. "Blue Ridge Mountain Blues" (1952) was Wade's first record since "Old Ruben" to feature his solo banjo; those from 1961 and thereafter routinely keep Wade's banjo up front in the bluegrass manner.

WADE I used a little open-back Bacon & Day on the first records we made. It was the only banjo I had until I got my new Gibson RB-5 in 1935 or '36. Fisher Hendley had a Gibson banjo and I played that one for a good long while, while I was at WBT in Charlotte for Crazy Water Crystals. He was from down in Albemarle, North Carolina, and he brought me his banjo to play on the air. It was a good banjo, same as mine is now. Around 1935 I had a new Whyte Laydie banjo, a gift from Crazy Water Crystals. People tell me it's one of the best sounding banjos they've ever heard, but [laughs] I think it's just my banjo playing that sounds so good! J.E. kept the banjo after we broke up.

Fisher Hendley's banjo has belonged to Earl Scruggs since the 1940s. Wade Mainer still plays his own 1933 Gibson RB-Granada Mastertone (serial # 9530-5). Stan Werbin of Elderly Instruments in Lansing, Michigan is, as the name implies, a dealer in rare stringed instruments. He has examined Wade's banjo and notes that:

Most prewar Mastertones had archtop tone rings, and his has the more desirable flathead tone ring. He took it back to the factory for some repair in the 1960s and when they gave it back to him all the original hardware (including the very valuable prewar flathead tone ring) was gone, replaced by 1960s RB-800 parts. They didn't ask him if he would like shiny new parts to replace the old dull ones. They just did it.

Similar to the story of why Bill Monroe scratched "The Gibson" out of the peghead of his mandolin—he had brought it to the factory for one thing and they did something else major without his permission. The folks at Gibson surely were not being malicious about either of these incidents, but they were evidently clueless about the fact that they were not making the instruments as well as they had earlier, and "upgrading" to new parts or finish (in the case of Monroe's mando) was just the plain wrong way to go.

Around 1990 the folks at Gibson became aware of what had happened to the banjo. The Granada had just been reissued by Gibson, so they had more appropriate parts to put back on it. Hence, although not original prewar metal parts, the new ones look far better than the RB-800 parts. (Personal communication, 26 June 2009)

away, until their insurance allowed them to purchase another house, this time with a backyard large enough to accommodate a big vegetable garden that Julia still cultivates.

Following the disaster Julia and Wade were resilient and resourceful, and they cheerfully picked up their lives and moved on. Friends and family pitched in, their music was still in demand, and they learned that a lot of people cared about them. They have never quite retired from music making, but they stay closer to home these days and play informally more than professionally. When Wade turned 100 on April 21, 2007, he and Julia played for more than an hour to a packed house at the Community Center in nearby Fenton, Michigan. He observed at the time that his 101st birthday would be anticlimactic, but he was wrong. To accommodate a larger crowd, the 2008 celebration was moved to a sports arena and four hundred fans were privileged to hear Wade and Julia once more.[2] On Saturday, April 18, 2009, the close-knit Mainer family (including daughter Polly and sons Frank, Kelly, and Randall) and fellow musicians Virgil Shouse and Mel Hammon hosted a 102nd birthday celebration at the Burton Senior Citizen Center in Michigan. When I concluded this account a few months later, plans were under way for the party in 2010.

Today Frank Mainer and his wife Eva live on the old family farm in Mocksville, where his grandparents lived and worked nearly a century ago. Polly and her husband Ralph Frederick have been to the house Wade built seventy years ago in Stony Knob. Ralph reports: "The house still stands; however, the acreage has been sold off by various owners over the years. Today there is a southern style diner on the lot next to the house which is a very popular breakfast spot. Polly and I have had Sunday breakfast there on at least one occasion, and it was excellent!"

NOTES

1. Earl Scruggs, *Earl Scruggs and the 5-String Banjo: Revised and Enhanced Edition*. Hal Leonard Corporation, 2005, 158.

2. Melissa Burden, "Wade Mainer performs 'beautiful, wonderful music' during 101st birthday party and concert," *The Flint Journal*, April 19, 2008 mlive.com/entertainment/flint/index.ssf/2008/04/wade_mainer_performs_beautiful.html.

Wade Mainer's Banjo Playing

"Nobody ever showed me anything on the banjo. I just stuck to what I got and I hung on to it."[1] At age 102, Wade Mainer speaks with candor about his sprawling musical past. Though he insists that "I don't have that much banjo learning," and judges his self-taught skills a product of tenacity more than talent, he has bequeathed to bluegrass an enduring repertory. He names a few of his contributions: "Little Maggie," "Dream of the Miner's Child," "Little Pal," "Uncloudy Day," and "Have a Little Talk with Jesus." In another conversation he brings up still more: "Maple on the Hill," "Take Me in the Lifeboat," and "Wreck on the Highway"—and this list can be much expanded.[2] Wade has served a pivotal role in their dissemination. For professionals and amateurs alike, his influence begins with the dark shellac records he made as a young man playing in a high-energy string band over the radio airwaves and reaches to the flatbed stages of today's outdoor festivals and the parking-lot sessions that run late into the night.

Wade's two-finger banjo playing figures both literally and emblematically in that continuity. For all its propulsive charm—"it is kind of a catchy tune," he says of the whole style—he also calls it "obsolete" and "old-fashioned."[3] He recognizes that few, if any, still play as he does. Nevertheless, his distinctive technique epitomizes a shift from an older string band sound to the bluegrass that succeeded it. In the 1930s he thrived as one of the only professional country musicians to perform with the five-string banjo on radio and recordings. If this choice of instrument seemed inherently archaic at that time, when country music had begun turning from its string band past toward a songwriter's craft, centered around a lead vocalist, his resonator banjo

BLUE MOUNTAIN BELLS

by WADE MAINER
Setting by RON SMOLKA

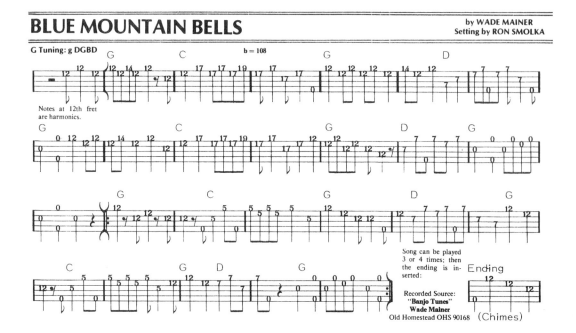

Tablature of 1984 instrumental "Blue Mountain Bells," reprinted with permission of Ron Smolka

and the picks that he placed on his forefinger and thumb gave signs of a corresponding modernity.

Like many youngsters playing the banjo in western North Carolina where he grew up, he initially learned the down-picking method. Sometimes called "frailing," "clawhammer" (Wade uses both terms), "rapping," or "knocking," the right hand produces notes with the fist loosely clenched, the nail of the index finger striking down on the string. The hand—outwardly shaped like the clawhammer part of a hammer—falls, while the thumb rests or else sounds the short fifth string. However, in the "drop-thumb" technique, the thumb alternates with the index finger, plucking down on another of the melody strings. This percussive style, long used in Wade's community, well suited the dance pieces and ballads that he and his neighbors enjoyed. But Wade, who learned to frail from family member Will Banks, found that the approach did not suit him. "It just seemed like the tunes didn't come out with that type of playing," Wade recalls. "I wanted to make the banjo understood, the tunes understood a little better."[4] He gravitated to other types of banjo picking that gave a more precise effect: "Sometimes when I'm playing a breakdown, I'll lead with my forefinger, and when I'm playing a ballad or a slow song, you know, sometimes I'll use my thumb. . . . The music had to fit the story being told."[5] In the forefinger style, the index finger darts from melody to accompaniment, setting up a rapid flow of notes, while the thumb lead is better able to control and shape a slower sequence. Wade's choice of fingering extends an old idea of a specific tuning forming an environment for a single tune. As he says, the music has to fit the story being told.

"It has a plunky, crisp sound," writes banjoist and collector Art Rosenbaum of the forefinger-lead method that Wade and his fellow North Carolinians Bascom Lunsford and Doc Watson so often employed. He adds that this style is used "to good advantage accompanying songs and ballads; but it can be made to sound hard and driving enough to work for dance tunes, particularly with other instruments. In brief, this is the idea: with the right hand braced on the head, the *index* finger alternates between the inside strings and the first, while the thumb plays the off-beats on the 5th string, also at times coming down to the 2nd string for double thumbing."[6]

The style emerges within a larger heritage. Throughout the banjo's development from a gourd strung with catgut to a burnished machine made of metal and wood, its players have devised an abundance of tunings. That made sense on the earliest banjos, which were homemade, fretless, and hard to note with accuracy along the fingerboard's upper reaches. Players could adjust the strings' individual pitches to fit a given tune. With a few moves—or sometimes none—on the fretboard, a melody becomes framed within the ringing strings that surround it. When Wade talks about his banjo playing, he tells this history by the notes of his banjo strings: "I tune in the key of D to play certain songs, songs like 'Old Reuben' and 'I've Always Been a Rambler.' Then I go into G for a faster, a more up date song. I go into C for a little higher singing, and I sometimes tune in F and E . . . for the long, drawn out songs, ballads."[7]

The D tuning that Wade mentions for "Old Reuben" (fifth string to first: f#DF#AD) proves so suited for this piece that the entire tune can be performed one-handed on open strings, without fretting a single note. Admittedly, most players, including Wade, do not leave this song to just one hand but play it on the neck in coordination with their picking, making it a showpiece. Still, the fit between "Reuben" and D tuning points to a wider phenomenon. Tunings have long provided a means to present an individual tune in its fullness. Not only do open strings hold a number of the principal melody notes, but the whole sound of the banjo comes to echo around the piece being played, an aesthetic that Wade's contemporary, Virginia banjoist Hobart Smith, called "playing the banjo for everything that's in it."[8] When Wade Mainer says that he plays certain songs, like "Reuben," in certain keys, he has alluded to this venerable practice that he first encountered as a youth.

Wade then mentions playing in G, which he further characterizes in terms of speed and modernity. By 1918, when he was eleven years old and found himself first drawn to the instrument, fretted, mail-order banjos had reached the western North Carolina mountains, where he and his family lived. The open-chord tuning of G (gDGBD), while already in use on fretless banjos, proved especially adaptable on these more recently manufactured instruments. The frets allowed players to explore the whole of the banjo neck with accurate intonation, making repeatable chord shapes possible across its length. Three-finger banjoists made particular use of this capacity, and with a capo and corresponding adjustments on the fifth string, the G tuning also allowed them to play in all keys. Yet even with this increased sophistication, mountain players hung on to the old sound, frequently situating their melodies in the midst of open-string drones.

Wade's 1984 instrumental "Blue Mountain Bells," illustrated by the accompanying tablature, brings this technique to life.[9] The piece mines the thematic pattern set by "Spanish Fandango" and "Chilly Winds," as well as Wade's "Laughing Song" and his "Tricklin' Waters." It makes full use of the neck, rising to its upper reaches, employing barre chords and harmonics. Wade could not have played "Blue Mountain Bells" on a mountaineer's fretless banjo. He needed a factory-made model to realize the tune's precision and execute its special effects. Drawn from the past, "Bells" now arose in a modern framework. Wade's colleagues did much the same as they developed their approaches to the instrument.

By the mid-1940s, banjo luminaries like Snuffy Jenkins and Earl Scruggs, who performed the bulk of their work in G, had effected, in historian Karen Linn's words, an "artful compromise."[10] They drew from a precedent in jazz to take instrumental breaks, and combined in their three-finger picking the arpeggios of ragtime virtuosos of the late nineteenth century and the full-neck chording typical of plectrum and tenor banjo soloists of the 1920s. Largely urban-bred and musically literate, the turn-of-the-century ragtime virtuosos, Linn writes, numbered among the earliest recording artists. Playing into the speaking funnel and cutting stylus of this new phonographic technology, they performed highly complex marches (such as "Stars and Stripes Forever"), many of the banjo's so-called "characteristic pieces," stressing the syncopated qualities of the recent ragtime compositions, and even arranged classical works that they played in a three-finger style. By the succeeding decade, another trend arose as plectrum and tenor banjoists began working in the new dance orchestras. This music demanded a largely rhythmic rather than melodic role for the banjo. Accordingly, these banjoists found the instrument's fifth string vestigial and removed it. They also replaced the gut strings and finger-style picking of the ragtime method with a mandolin-type plectrum scraped across their substantially louder steel strings to gain needed volume. Their solos, based on chords and chord-melody breaks, suited the popular dances of the jazz era. Country musicians like Earl Scruggs came in contact with these developments, which, as Linn explains, he and his colleagues artfully adapted to their own sensibilities.

Wade Mainer likewise brought an updated sound to his version of mountain music. As a member of the first generation to learn from electric media, he and his band members responded to contemporary recordings of traditional songs with their own records, stamping them with their signature artistry. Wade's early recordings show him performing both moody ballads and forceful hoedowns in one or another of his banjo styles. For example, his 1937 "Wild Bill Jones" uses a thumb lead, while his 1941 recording of "Old Hen She Cackled" uses the index finger to drive the piece. As his interests centered primarily on songs and vocal arrangements, he played abbreviated, though assertive, banjo breaks on his records. Rather than devise leads from the chord positions that Scruggs and others soon developed, or as he says, "cut it up or jazz it up," Wade used a spare economy of notes, essentially linear melodic shapes fit within an insistent, rhythmic framework.[11] Even though a number of his recordings feature his banjo prominently, he considered the fiddle the principal instrumental vehicle for this idiom: "Fiddle was the lead instrument, you know, on down 'til you run down to bluegrass."[12]

Wade's "up date" songs refer back to the G tuning. When he next cites the C tuning for some higher-pitched singing, he implicitly includes the unique qualities this setting makes available. Wade actually employs two separate C tunings, each with their own dictates and traditions. The first, which he calls "double C" (gCGCD), has long figured in mountain practice. Wade accordingly uses it for such traditional mountain numbers as "Shout Little Luly," "Cindy," and "Little Birdie." He also uses a C tuning usually called "standard C" (gCGBD). This tuning, documented in the earliest of the antebellum banjo tutors, presents a different set of possibilities from either G tuning or double C. Less confined harmonically than an open-chord or a modal tuning, by the nineteenth century's end it allowed sophisticated banjoists (like ragtime recording artists) to speak of "scientific playing"—an approach they employed in this C tuning that combined the rigors of written music with technically difficult passages from both popular and classical music. Although Wade names C tuning here in his capacity as a singer, his use of it reveals a larger inheritance at work.

Banjo method books, sheet music, and cylinder recordings show that ragtime and earlier minstrel-show players repeatedly used the standard C tuning. (In minstrelsy it was tuned to a lower pitch, but kept the same relationship of notes.) Beginning in the 1830s, and continuing for the next fifty years, blackface banjo minstrelsy became the most popular stage entertainment in the United States, eventually giving way to vaudeville and the ethnic theater. In the rural Southeast where Wade lived, minstrelsy extended to the twentieth-century medicine show, and Wade performed in bands that included blackface comedy. For mountain players like himself, the standard C tuning not only transmitted songs from that past but offered new technical possibilities. Wade called on it, for example, in his 1941 performance of "Arkansas Traveler," a celebrated comic piece that combines musicianship with humor. Other North Carolina banjoists like Charlie Poole had earlier recorded "Dixie" in this setting; Poole credited it to Yankee rag and march specialist Fred Van Eps, while Tennessee players Sam and Kirk McGee likewise situated the bulk of their neck-spanning banjo marches in this key. Before the ascendancy of G tuning, standard C provided a system of chord shapes and bass runs well equipped to meet the new virtuoso styles gaining the attention of rural banjoists.

As a young musician Wade found it necessary to cope with the impact that the C and G tunings had among his peers. Soon after he dropped frailing, he started learning a three-finger style akin to Charlie Poole's. But when he played that method with his older brother, fiddler J.E. Mainer, the siblings found it did not fit their combination. "It wouldn't suit our kind of music," said Wade. "The time was off."[13] J.E. prevailed upon Wade to use a two-finger method, better suited to follow his long-bow fiddling and the rhythm it required. The emerging bluegrass music called for still another timing, and Wade admits that both he and Snuffy Jenkins, who later played with J.E., "had his problems with the banjo just like me."[14] In moving into this newer style, Jenkins "changed the banjo timin' from old time to bluegrass time."[15] One result of this change, Wade concluded, was an emphasis on musical technique rather than song content. "Bluegrass, to me, is show music instead of listening music."[16]

Wade's stance returns us to the tunings and all they imply. What he intends becomes clear when he speaks of playing in E and F for his "long, drawn out songs, ballads." For either one he will "tune the music way up high"—literally tightening all the strings—or else, "hook 'em up," meaning use a capo, or a "clamp" as he terms it, to reach these keys.[17] Whether he clamps on a capo or tightens his strings, his pitch adjustments amount to variations on his C, D, and G tunings. Rather than seeking out the flexible, chord-based opportunities that bluegrass banjo in G affords the modern player, or that standard C offered an earlier generation of players, he cleaves to an even older welding of sound and sense, tuning and tune. By conceiving of these keys as tunings, and playing these pieces in that tradition, he fits the music to the story being told, shaping the drawn-out ballads according to an old-time aesthetic.

Like a cutaway in a side of earth, Wade Mainer's playing reveals an archaeology of the banjo, from his picking styles to his tunings. Over the course of his wondrously long life, a life that began over a century ago in Buncombe County, North Carolina, he has seen epochs of musical change. He has lived so long, he once told me, that the music even changed its name, turning from "from mountain to hillbilly to old-time," yet all of it still pertaining to one thing only: "true country music."[18] The first label, "mountain," tells of a regional style, enclaved and remote. The second, "hillbilly," brings an awareness of commercial markets, an industrialization of a formerly home music. Finally, "old-time" denotes how this body of true country music has aged, appreciated nowadays by many outside the culture where it began. All the same he issues a caution, knowing the risks of hardened categories: "Please say 'to the best of my knowledge, as best as I can remember, this is the way it was for me.' I don't know nothing about music."[19] While conscious of the frailties of memory and ever modest about his knowledge, Wade Mainer gives witness to his times. He remembers mountain music and the life that surrounded it, and he survives as the last hillbilly recording artist. The oldest of the old-time musicians, when Wade says, "I try to play it as plain as I can," he defines the lasting appeal behind his decades of music-making.[20]

—STEPHEN WADE
July 2009

NOTES

1. Wade Mainer interview with Stephen Wade, April 27, 2009.

2. See Ron Smolka, "Wade Mainer Bridging the Gap: 2-Finger to 3-Finger Style," *Banjo Newsletter* 12 no. 2 (December 1984): 6.

3. Wade Mainer interview, April 27, 2009.

4. Smolka, 5.

5. Thomas Warlick, "Two Fast Fingers: Wade Mainer," *Banjo Newsletter* 30 no. 4 (February 2003): 24.

6. Art Rosenbaum, *Old-Time Mountain Banjo* (New York: Oak, 1968): 33. Italics as in original.

7. Smolka, 6.

8. See Stephen Wade's notes to Hobart Smith, *In Sacred Trust: The 1963 Fleming Brown Tapes*, Smithsonian Folkways SFW CD 40141 (2005): 17.

9. Thanks to Ron Smolka and to *Banjo Newsletter* editors Donald and Spencer Nitchie for permission to reprint his tablature of "Blue Mountain Bells."

10. Karen Linn, *That Half-Barbaric Twang* (Urbana: University of Illinois Press, 1991): 142.

11. Warlick, 24

12. *Ibid.*

13. Smolka, 5.

14. Warlick, 25.

15. *Ibid.*

16. *Ibid.*

17. Wade Mainer interview, April 27, 2009.

18. Wade Mainer interview with Stephen Wade, July 26, 1999.

19. *Ibid.*

20. Smolka, 6.

MAINERS, MONROES, AND BLUEGRASS

WADE [In 1935] the Monroe Brothers had just come into North Carolina. They was a little hard to get acquainted with; they didn't just come right out and talk to you. Charlie would, but Bill wouldn't say much. When I was on WPTF in Raleigh, I drew more mail than Charlie and Bill did, and I think they were a little bit jealous. They didn't stay there; they left the station. They weren't getting mail and they didn't draw when they went on personal appearances. They didn't fill much more than half the house when they'd go out to these schoolhouses where we were doing two and three shows. The Monroes kept to themselves and didn't think much of our music. Byron Parker was with them for a while. When he left them, they went down—didn't nobody like 'em. They were pretty good ol' boys, but they didn't mess with us much and we didn't mess with them. We drew more listeners than they did. They had little songbooks but people didn't buy them. They weren't on WPTF very long; I guess we were too much competition.

They worked everywhere trying to get their music the way they wanted it. They got into that high-pitched tuning and singing—in overdrive, I'll put it that way. They came out with one song that I recorded [2/14/1936] just before they did [2/17/1936], "What Would You Give in Exchange for Your Soul." I've heard this, that they told

RCA Victor that [the Monroes would defect] if they let Wade Mainer's record come out.

One time I happened to do a number people had requested, "Motherless Children Has a Hard Time in This Old World." First thing I knew, Charlie came into the station, came up to me, sat there and waited till I came off the air. Then he come up to me and said, "Wade, I don't want you playing that song anymore." I said, "Is it your song?" He said, "No, I didn't write it but I sing it all the time."

"Well," I said, "I'll keep on singing it as long as the people want it." He turned around and said, "Well, I'll just whup you all over the place." I said, "You might do that, Charlie, but you'll find out that I've been there." From then on there was never a hard word [between us].

Bill asked me one time to play with him, back when he pulled away from Charlie. I said, "Bill, I don't play your kind of music. It's too fast for me." I believe he went and got Stringbean. Bill didn't have a bluegrass band then, and Charlie didn't either. They tell me I was a trailblazer for bluegrass music; I made it easy for those who came after me. They picked it all up and it swept the country. Bill worked hard and turned it around. Clyde Moody worked some with him and said, "Wade, that man's the hardest man to work for you ever seen. If you missed a practice, he'd bawl you out."

When them boys got to playing back there, Earl Scruggs wasn't the only boy that played with three fingers. He played with the Morris Brothers for a while. When Bill Monroe got started [he] named his band the Blue Grass Boys. He did hear some of my banjo playing, I'm pretty sure of that. He was looking for a banjo player and he got with Stringbean, [and] he worked with Stringbean for quite some time. I don't know how Bill changed to go into B flat or C or D. That changed the old-time music altogether, and the banjo players was playing [with] three fingers. If you'll notice, they're not in good time all the time.

You know, those boys, they were good in their way of playing and singing. I liked the music, I listened to it every chance I'd get. Their timing in a lot of their music, I could hear it. If they were doing a song that I knowed, I could hear the timing and mistakes and all like that. I heard Bill play so fast that you didn't know what he was playin', but they had good timing! I guess everyone to their own taste. Bill wouldn't hardly have got nowhere at all without a banjo player. Stringbean sounded pretty good, even when he was doing comedy. If you listen to Earl, he . . . well, he's a banjo player, I'll just put it that way. I don't say he's all that good but, when he got with Bill Monroe, why then he went places.

I was pretty well acquainted with Bill. Bill and I was good friends before the Lord called the old boy and took him home. I hope he made it to Heaven. I'll give Bill credit; he done a good job and really brought the music that people talk about today.

Wade's mixed feelings about the Monroes are understandable. The latter were groundbreaking musicians whose unwelcome competition came at a time when both groups were in ascendance. As he correctly perceives, Bill and Charlie performed at rapid tempos and pitched their voices and instruments higher than usual, introducing stylistic changes that set them apart from the Mainers, Carters, and Blue Sky Boys. These changes persisted and evolved into the high energy ensemble music that Bill and Charlie introduced in 1938–39 with their respective new bands. Bill's fortunes advanced with his permanent Opry engagement in 1939 and his legendary 1945-48 Blue Grass Boys that included Lester Flatt and Earl Scruggs; the latter's virtuoso three-finger banjo picking style was novel and exciting, and countless young musicians sought to imitate him.

As noted, Wade had developed his own original style based on two-finger picking, but it sounded enough like Earl's to confuse casual listeners.

PHOTOS, LETTERS, AND MEMORIES

W.J. and Polly Mainer family photo, c. 1912. L to R: Gertrude, Eva, Willis, W.J., Essie, Wade, Finley, Polly, J.E., James.

WADE We were a poor family but in our hearts and our living and in the ways of God they taught us something. My family was all Christians. My older brothers and sisters left home when I was still a small boy, and I don't know too much about them after that.

Back during the Depression you couldn't find work and you had to get out and get on your own. It happened that Papa had a little farm and we raised all of our stuff to live on. During the wintertime my dad would dig a hole in the ground and cover food to keep through the winter. If we wanted anything he'd buried, apples, potatoes and things like that, we'd go out, get what we wanted, bring it in, and Mama would cook it on the stove. All told, I think he was working about fifteen acres. He had a mule and a turning plow and a bull-tongue plow. He hitched the mule to the plow and worked in the garden—no gasoline engines nowhere 'round!

Julia Mae Brown, mid-1930s

Julia as Hillbilly Lillie, ca. 1935.

WADE In 1935 I met Miss Julia Brown when we were on WBT in Charlotte. She was a singer and musician, playing part time over WSJS in Winston-Salem. Julia's father was a farmer, and he listened to the Mountaineers' morning program. Julia and her mother decided to give her father a surprise birthday party, if we were available. Our book keeper had the date open and arrangements were made. This is where I first met Julia.

We continued on WBT for a while, and then went to WPTF in Raleigh, North Carolina. During this time I corresponded with Julia and, when we did not have a show date on Saturday night, I would drive approximately a hundred miles to see her.

Frank Hall Brown and daughter
Julia Mae, 1930s.

Julia at home, 1930s.

Julia Mae Brown publicity photo, 1930s.

Hallowe'en costume, 1930s.

Julia, 1930s.

Julia at home with Jack, 1930s.

JULIA MAE BROWN MAINER

W.J. and Polly Mainer,
ca. 1940.

JULIA I found the old guitar down at my grandpa's in North Carolina where I went to visit a lot. It kind of fascinated me. I got interested and tried to play it—didn't know nothin' about it! When I was a teenager I still liked the guitar, and my dad bought me one, a Kalamazoo. I sent down to Nashville, Tennessee for a songbook that had guitar chords in it. I learned some chords and just started pickin' from there. I took lessons on the piano but I liked the guitar better. My uncle M. G. Brown was a fire chief in Winston-Salem. He came over to visit my dad, and he heard me pickin' and singin' there at the house. He said, "Julia, I think you're good enough to be on the radio."

That just kind of struck a chord with me, so I aggravated my dad until he took me over there to Winston-Salem, and there's where I got onto WSJS radio in 1934. I tried out and they said I was OK. Dad took me over there

whenever he had the opportunity. It was around twenty-six miles from home, and I wasn't regularly scheduled. It came to an end right after I met Wade—I don't think I broadcast too many times after that. We lived on a farm in Mocksville, North Carolina. The farm had quite a few acres, I don't recall exactly how many. Dad had horses and hired help. Back then you'd have to have a mule or two to pull the plow. He had a tractor in later years until he finally gave up farming.

Dad, he got up early and he listened to the Mainer Mountaineers in the morning. He really liked their program, so Mom and I we got together for Dad's birthday in 1935. We talked it over and decided to get them to come up and surprise him. We sent them a letter and they had the date open, so they said they would come. We made arrangements and they came up.

Wade with mother-in-law Julia Rowena Brown, Weaverville, NC, ca. 1940.

Julia Rowena Brown in her front yard, Mocksville, NC, ca. 1940.

Brown family home place, date unknown.

It was about one o'clock that day when I had a program. Mama told me to keep Dad in town as long as I could because Wade and J.E. were coming in that afternoon. So after I got off the radio we went to a ball game. When it was getting late, Dad wanted to come home because he had some chores to do. I tried to keep him but I couldn't. When we got home Mama said, "We got to keep Dad away from here," because the band hadn't shown up yet. Dad had some hired hands, so we sent one of them out to have him get Dad to town. They went, and when he came back it was a big surprise—and there's where I first met Wade.

The couple survived a long-distance courtship while the band took to the road. They were married in 1937 (shortly before Julia made her only pre-1961 appearance on record) and

have balanced music-making and family-raising ever since. Ever the trouper, she pitched in to help the band in 1937 and 1938, handling bookings and ticket sales. In 1939 she retired from music to start a family, reappeared to sing with Wade in church meetings in the 1950s, and recorded with him again in 1961. Had she chosen to pursue her own music career, she would have ranked with Wilma Lee, Kitty Wells, and Molly O'Day in the 1940s, when young, talented female singers were beginning to carve out a significant place in country music. When Wade began to perform again after retiring from his day job in 1972, Julia joined him on stage and records for a family music partnership that continues to this day.

WADE She just has to get in a certain key that she can sing in, and she has a voice. It's a beautiful voice, don't ever hear nobody else sing with a voice like she sings with.

Julia Rowena Brown with grandson Randall Mainer (b. June 25, 1955) on the Brown family farm.

Julia Mae Mainer.

Brown home (winter), 1930s.

Brown home (summer), 1930s.

J.E. (left) and Wade, near Charlotte, mid-1930s.

Wade at Julia Brown's home, Mocksville, 1930s.

MAINERS' MOUNTAINEERS, THE 1930s

WADE We were country. We were poor folk but we were country. We played ballads, old songs, gospel music, mountain songs, and things like that. I learned a lot of songs off of Gid Tanner and the Skillet Lickers and Charlie Poole, Riley Puckett, Clayton McMichen, the Piedmont Log Rollers. When we did, we had to buy the record and take it home to learn the tune on it. We had a phonograph and we bought their records and learned a whole lot of their songs, but our music was still different from theirs. We stuck to the old-timey good listening music.

When J.E. and I got together in Concord, North Carolina, we worked at a cotton mill and practiced music in our spare time. We'd go out on Saturdays to help people with their crops, playing music for corn shuckings, bean pulling and candy making parties. Then they'd have a big roast—we learned a whole lot of music like that.

When we were still working in the cotton mill we had the Lay brothers, who worked there too. We got our band going and got a program on WSOC in Gastonia. We had to work, we had to rehearse night and day. One time I was working in the cotton mill, J.E. came in when I was taking a nap before going to work on the night shift, J.E. woke me and said, "Get up, get up, get up!" I said, "What's the matter, J.E.?" Says, "I just learned a new tune on my fiddle—I want you to get your banjo." I think it might have been "Train Number 111." He made it sound like the steam [evaporating], going down the mountain, and that's where the famous bluegrass song came from, "Orange Blossom Special"—they learned that from us. Ollie Bunn done the same thing with his fiddle on "New Lost Train Blues." They're the ones that started that quivering peck, peck, peck with their bows to get that train sound on the music. We broke the trail for other musicians and made it easy for them.

Anybody would be glad to play with J.E., 'cause he had such a good time with that fiddle, and you don't hear that kind of fiddling any more. You could understand what he was doing, "Lee Highway Blues," "Train Number 111," and all. To me, he was the best. He had good time, he didn't chop his music, he didn't play fast, and he didn't rock his bow when he was playing. He played the song like it ought to be played, and you could understand the song. I don't know of anyone else that's ever played with a long bow who played like he did. There was a lot of good fiddlers, don't get me wrong. There was fiddlers out there that could fiddle a ring around him, far as that goes. But his time and his

Wade Mainer, early 1930s.

JULIA That's where you worked in Concord.
WADE Yeah, that was a Gibson and I was at the cotton mill.

music and the long bow—no, I don't think I remember anybody that I ever heard play like that.

I loved his old banjo playing. He wasn't a frailer, but he done pretty good with some of the songs, you know. We just tuned our instruments up in G or C or D, whatever key we wanted to play in, and we would play in that key. We didn't go up there in high C or high B and sing it out [with] the band drowning out the music.

In putting the Mainer Mountaineers together we tried out several boys that had good timing and good voices. This is how we got acquainted with Zeke Morris: his brother George was at a picnic and I was there, so me and George got the guitar and banjo and sang a song or two for the people. He agreed to give us another test with my brother J.E. But when we went to find George we found Zeke, his brother. I tried Zeke out; we took him up on the side of the hill and played little bit, and I thought we done pretty good. We took him back with us and practiced and rehearsed and I think we made a good choice. Our duet singing and playing had a different sound. We got another guitar player, John Love. He was a blues singer who sung like Jimmie Rodgers and yodeled a lot. He didn't make all that many recordings with us, but he made some by himself.

Then it was J.E.'s band; I was just his brother playing banjo in the band. Fisher Hendley came over to the mill where we were working and wanted to talk to us. We went down there and met him at the gate. He said, "I want you to come over to Charlotte and play some music with us." We went over and took an audition and Crazy Water Crystals hired us just like that. We went to our boss man and told him we wanted to get off for two or three weeks to see how it was going to turn out, after that they wanted to hire us full time. We went to the boss and told him and he said, "Well, you boys go right ahead. If it fails, your job will be waiting on you when you get back." I joined the American Federation of Musicians when WBT was growing big, you know. They sent me a card and I paid up. I gave it up when I moved up here to Michigan.

We played at WBT for quite some time, and they wanted to send us down to New Orleans to work for Crazy Water Crystals at station WWL. We were there for about a month and people wanted to know where the Mainer Mountaineers went to, and they had to tell 'em that we were down there on another station. So they began to holler and cry for us, and Crazy Water Crystals had to bring us back.

Publicity photo, mid-30s.

COMPLIMENTS OF "THE CRAZY COMPANY"
Broadcasting Daily 12:00 Noon over WWNC
(Except Saturday and Sunday)
Also

| WWNC Asheville | CRAZY BARN DANCE WBT—Charlotte Every Saturday Night For | WWNC Asheville |

THE CRAZY CO.
CHARLOTTE, N. C.

Publicity photo, mid-30s.

L to R: Fisher Hendley (announcer), Daddy John Love, Wade, Zeke Morris, J.E., WBT, 1934. The promotional card is from WWNC, where the Mountaineers appeared on daily noon shows in 1934–35, noting that they were also featured on WBT Saturday nights. Wade admired Hendley's banjo, a 1933 Gibson RB-Granada Mastertone (serial #9584-3), and soon acquired one of his own (9530-5), that he still owns. Historians claim that fewer than 20 banjos with five-string necks like theirs were made. The Hendley banjo later belonged to Snuffy Jenkins and Don Reno before winding up in the hands of Earl Scruggs, who played it on "Foggy Mountain Breakdown" in 1949, and virtually all his records since.

WPTF souvenir book, 1935. L to R: Zeke Morris, J.E. Mainer, Byron
Parker (Uncle Tom), Wade Mainer, Boyden Carpenter (The Hillbilly Kid).

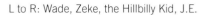
L to R: Wade, Zeke, the Hillbilly Kid, J.E.

The Mountaineers Open Their Daily Mail

The above picture shows only a part of the many thousands of letters and telegrams received during a four months' period from you our loyal friends and listeners. As the boys rummage through this pile of mail it is no wonder their faces express delight, for indeed this is a flattering stack of mail for any group. It is your response by these telegrams and letters, and your regular use of "Crazy" Water Crystals, and "Crazy" Water Fiz that makes these programs possible, and we wish to thank you from the bottom of our hearts for your generous response by letters, telegrams and your purchases of "Crazy" Water Crystals, this grand old product of Mother Nature. We take a keen delight in advertising such a worthy product with our music and song, for on our regular daily programs and on the "Crazy" Barn Dance program on

Saturday night we not only give you music and good clean entertainment, but when "Uncle Tom" talks to you about "Crazy" Water Crystals, we feel that we are truly offering a helping hand to suffering humanity. We very much appreciate your many compliments of our programs, and the wonderful things you have had to say about the product which we represent, and we trust that you will continue to send us your requests for these programs though the quantity of mail now received daily makes it necessary to eliminate personal dedications on the programs. Just remember that our programs are made up by your requests, and although we cannot call your name in personal dedication, your letter or postal card contributes greatly to the placing of your favorite number on the program.

Wade *and* Zeke

This popular Hillbilly Duet was formed by accident about a year ago in J. E. Mainer's Crazy Mountaineers Group, and has fast developed into one of the most popular Hillbilly duets in the South and were so dubbed by R C A Victor Company for whom they have made many recordings on Blue Bird Records. It is hard to pick the most popular of the songs which these boys sing, but we must rate at the top of the rank the song "Maple On The Hill" which these two boys themselves made popular, and though it is now heard on practically every radio station, and by all Hillbilly groups, we think you will agree with us in the statement, that no one will ever sing it quite so well as Wade and Zeke.

Wade and Zeke's "Maple On the Hill" was recorded as a duet, and it was the hit from the 1935 session. In 1936 the pair began to hold separate sessions in addition to performing on those led by J.E.

The Crazy Mountaineers

Quoting the words of "Uncle Tom"—"The many thousands of our regular listeners have joined with R C A Victor in declaring this group one of the best Hillbilly bands ever to broadcast from any station." These boys have made many Blue Bird Records for R C A Victor which have been among their best sellers. At the present time, they are heard daily with "Uncle Tom" on station WPTF and on the "Crazy" Barn Dance every Saturday night bringing you the health and happiness program sponsored by the Crazy Water Hotel Company of Mineral Wells, Texas. The boys are standing left to right: J. E. Mainer and the Hillbilly Kid. At the foot of the microphone, left to right: Zeke Morris and Wade Mainer. On the following pages you will find the words to many of the songs featured on the daily programs and the "Crazy" Barn Dance broadcast by the "Crazy" Mountaineers, J. E., Wade and Zeke, and Boyden Carpenter the "Hillbilly Kid." These are the songs which you have voted the most popular on our programs, and now that you have the words, why not just get the "Souvenir Book" and sing right along with us when we come to your house by radio.

COMING IN PERSON
THE
MAINER BROTHERS
AND THE
MOUNTAINERS

J. E. Mainer   Wade Mainer

AT

Harmony School

Saturday Night October 20th

DON'T MISS THE BIG STAGE SHOW
SAMBO and LIZAR
IN WHAT HAPPEN ON WASH DAY
With Lots of Old Time Playing and Singing
QUARTET - DUET - TRIO

Sponsored by School
Show Starts 7:30 P. M.

ADMISSION: Children 30c Adults 60c Inc. Tax
HEARD DAILY ON (W S J S) WINSTON-SALEM
11:30 A. M. and 1 till 2 P. M

1935.

WADE That was J.E.'s doing. When he come and got with me, he got me to do this stuff. I didn't like it and it didn't go over. We done it once or twice and then we didn't do it any more.

SOUTHERN RADIO CORPORATION
CHARLOTTE, N. C.

April 27, 1937

<u>TO ALL RADIO BROADCASTING STATIONS</u>

During the past three years the group known as Wade & Zeke have been the most outstanding Bluebird recording artists of the hillbilly type that this section of the country has ever had.

Their sensational record "Maple On The Hill" sold 53,000 copies for us. Each additional release of their recordings have sold remarkably well.

It is to my personal knowledge that they drew more fan mail over Radio Station WBT, Charlotte, N.C. than any other artists.

Very truly yours,

V. H. Sills, Mrg.
RECORD DEPT.
SOUTHERN RADIO CORP

Wade & Zeke endorsement from RCA distributor, 1937.

L to R: Wade, Robert (Buck) Banks, Maurice (Buddy) Banks, Chubby Overcash, summer 1937.

WADE I wasn't married yet. These are my sister's boys, Buck, Buddy Banks, and their friend Chubby Overcash. They were called the Little Smilin' Rangers, and they worked with me quite a while. They went back to school in the fall; then I organized the Sons of the Mountaineers. J.E. took Buck and Buddy down to Del Rio, Texas, and they stayed at a radio station down there for about six months.

Buddy (L) and Buck a few years later. A couple of J.E. Mainer's transcribed 1941 broadcasts with Buck and Buddy are included on the CD set Early Country Radio (JSP 7757).

SONS OF THE MOUNTAINEERS, 1937–1941

WADE When J.E. and me parted we were good friends, but I wasn't seeing things as good as he was. We got to where we couldn't see eye to eye; I had my way and he had his. We never had a fuss or a fight, but he drank most of the time and I couldn't take it. He wasn't a mean drunk, but he'd just spend everything he got.

We weren't making any money when we were broadcasting for Crazy Water Crystals. I told him I thought we could do a little better, but he didn't want to leave. At that time they were paying us at WBT [in Charlotte] and letting us make all the personal appearances that we could. The crowd would always have numbers they'd want us to play. We'd do those after the show was over. We got a lot of songs through people writing them down. A lot of those old songs would come from out of the mountains. If we didn't know a song and they requested it on the air we'd say we didn't know it and ask them to send us the words so we could try to put it together. I'd put my own music to the words, mostly. I didn't know how to read music, not one note from another one. We began to grow in our music and got to putting out some literature and writing a few songbooks. We weren't making much money from them; we were making it all on personal appearances. After the records started coming out back in '35 we sold records right and left. Everybody that heard us on the air bought one of our records.

I left Crazy Water Crystals in 1937 while we were on WPTF and I got the idea to form my own band. We were still brothers and we loved one another. We helped each other record some after that, but me and Zeke teamed up together. Homer Sherrill worked with us some, but he didn't stay too long. He recorded some songs with us, some hymns and all. Steve Ledford lived way back in the mountains in Bakersville, North Carolina. His dad played an old-time fiddle too. They came to see our show, just him and his dad. Steve brought a fiddle with him; after he saw the show, he said, "I play a fiddle a little bit." I said, "How would you like to play a tune or two with us?" So that's when we struck off. See, J.E. played with a long bow and he done a lot of them train songs. So we were looking for somebody to play with a long bow. He [Steve] played a lot like Fiddlin' John Carson when he got to playing solo and all. That's where we come up with that "Train 45," and made such a big hit.

J.E. would come to our house out of work and I'd give him a job. I hired J.E. because he was down and out, but I made a mistake doing that because I already had Steve Ledford, and there was friction between the two fiddlers. I didn't need 'em both and I was doin' it as a favor. Finally I just pulled away from the whole business and formed my own band, the Sons of the Mountaineers. George Morris got with J.E.'s band. He went with J.E. for a long time, I guess, him and a boy named Handsome [Leonard Stokes], and Snuffy Jenkins.

Morris and Stokes recorded over a dozen brother-style duets with their own guitar and mandolin accompaniments that were released under J.E.'s name in 1937, even though he didn't perform on them. DeWitt "Snuffy" Jenkins was an influential three-finger banjo stylist whose music inspired Don Reno and Earl Scruggs, among others. He played on just four titles with J.E. in 1937. In 1938, J.E. took the band to WIS in Columbia, South Carolina, where Byron Parker was the announcer. Parker had appeared in 1934 with the Mainers at WBT in Charlotte. When J.E. parted ways with his band in 1939, Parker assumed nominal leadership, hiring Homer Sherrill to play fiddle in J.E's place, and renamed the band Byron Parker's Mountaineers. Later they became the Hired Hands, in honor of Parker's on-air nickname, "The Old Hired Hand."

Mail pile at WPTF, 1937–38. Standing, L to R: Jay Hugh Hall, Clyde Moody. Kneeling, L to R: Wade Mainer, Steve Ledford.

WPTF, 1937–38. Standing, L to R: Wade Mainer, Steve Ledford. Kneeling, L to R: Clyde Moody, Jay Hugh Hall.

1937–38. L to R: Wade Mainer, Jay Hugh Hall, Clyde Moody, Steve Ledford.

WADE I was really thrilled and that's why I'm smiling. The way the people accepted me and my band on the air. Clyde Moody was a replacement for Zeke Morris. At the time a sponsor wanted to present another band in my time spot at 5:30 in the morning and have the station move us to another place on the schedule. Graham Pointer, WPTF's manager, came to me one day and he said, "Wade, we'll put it to a test and see if people still want you on the early program instead of the later one. You go out for personal appearances and sometimes you don't hardly get in the studio in time to do the program, and it might be nice if you wanted to move to another spot." I said, "Mr. Graham, it's your station. We're getting along good, people like us, and I'd like to stay on. Why don't we do this: why don't we announce it for two or three days?" If people wanted us to stay on at 5:30 we asked them to drop us a card. We got complaints from the farmers, cotton growers, and the tobacco growers who got up at 5 in the morning and were having breakfast while we were playing music. We won by five thousand and some few letters and the station decided to leave us on there. Before we were on they would be out somewhere or another feeding their horses and mules and getting ready to go to work. Then they'd come in, sit down and eat breakfast—and that's the time that we were on. Those radios were all battery sets—people didn't have electricity.

WADE MAINER
AND THE SONS OF THE MOUNTAINEERS

HOW DO YOU DO
EVERYBODY?
HOW DO YOU DO?

▼

J. E. Mainer, Steve
Ledford, Bill & Joe
and their singing
Guitars.

▼

Broadcast over Station
W. P. T. F.
Daily at 11:45

Presenting the Show

THE WEDDING OF
EFFIE MAE and
STEVE
and also
CORKEY

▼

Plenty of good old-time
hymn singing the way
you like to hear them
sung.

The trick of the steel strings—a nice, clean, show everybody will enjoy!
COME AND BRING YOUR FAMILY, AND ENJOY YOURSELF
FOR AN HOUR AND A HALF!
You have heard these boys over several Radio Stations thruout the South
NOW IS YOUR CHANCE TO SEE THEM IN PERSON AT
ELEM. SANVILLE SCHOOL
7 MI. W. OF BASSET, VA.
Sponsored by the School
SATURDAY, APR. 29 8:00 P.M.

1939 poster with "Bill & Joe."

WADE That was Jay Hugh Hall and Clyde Moody. I named them Bill and Joe on my program. They had played a little music before they got with me. The wedding show was just a little act that we got together. I'd play Corky. I wasn't in blackface; I didn't work in blackface for a good long while. We'd tell little jokes and stories, real nice and clean. A family could enjoy it—just good music, singing,

and friendship, that's what happened. It'd take about thirty minutes to do the little sketch for the children. The rest of the program was gospel and country music.

JULIA Right after we were married I would sell tickets, collect the money, and gave the school their part.

WADE That was one-third after the bills and all were paid, including posters and advertisements.

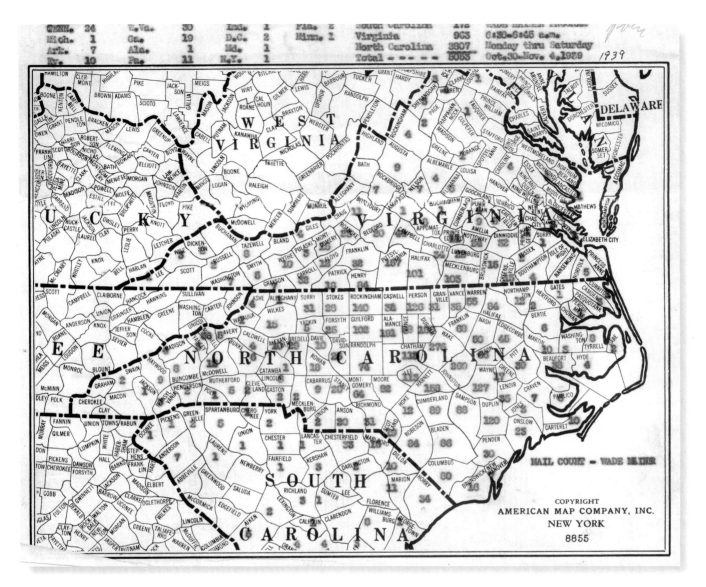

WPTF map with mail count by county, 1939.

Mail received during one week in the autumn of 1939, with distribution of listeners in each county of three states and other responders from Florida to Minnesota. The show aired at sunrise, later on WPTF's schedule than it had the year before, but still early enough to be heard at a distance.

WADE On WPTF those tobacco and cotton farmers wrote in and said they enjoyed us. They said that we were the only ones they listened to. They got up at five o'clock and listened to us at breakfast time. At the station they said that each letter meant that there were ten people listening.

August 20th, 1941

Mr. Wade Mainer,
Wade Mainer's "Sons Of The Mountaineers",
Station WWNC,
ASHEVILLE, NORTH CAROLINA

Dear Wade:

As you know, between July 15th and July 30th
WWNC offered to send its listeners a picture
of your organization if those listeners would
write the station requesting it. - And, brother,
they really wrote!

In 12 days you received 8,619 pieces of mail
requesting your picture. And that doesn't
include your regular fan-mail which has averaged
over 3,000 pieces a month. I think that this
response is really sensational. As a matter of
fact, the response to the picture offer has
definitely proved that your program is heard
by hundreds of thousands of people in 33 counties
located in North Carolina, South Carolina, and
Tennessee.

All in all, Wade, is just bears out the fact
that the "Sons Of The Mountaineers" is probably
the most popular hill-billy outfit we've had on
WWNC. It IS a swell outfit, - and you're entitled
to 'go places' with it!

My best wishes and a sincere 'thank you' are
certainly very much a part of this note to you.

Sincerely,

Promotion Director
STATION WWNC

Herman I. Moseley

1941 letter from WWNC to Wade.

MEMBER MUTUAL BROADCASTING SYSTEM

December 13, 1940

To Whom It May Concern:

Wade Mainer and the Sons of the Mountaineers
drew 729 pieces of mail on 4 spot announce-
ments offering a picture give away.

Yours very truly
Radio Station WAIR

C. G. Hill
Commercial Manager

CGH:gfb

WINSTON-SALEM ♦ NORTH CAROLINA
"Do Not Underestimate Your Invisible Audience"

1940 WAIR endorsement.

Two Royal Crown photos, WAIR Winston-Salem, 10 December 1940.

WADE There was a fellow on that station, his name was Reed Wilson who was one of the best announcers anywhere. He was playing records, any kind of music. He worked the early program and the night program. He was popular, and he got to poppin' off two or three times, telling the station that I was getting more publicity than he was. They said why don't we run a contest and see who's who and who ain't. There were four of us in the competition, so they set up little wooden horses and made them like a race track. They moved them according to the mail we each got. Reed Wilson and I stayed in there but the others dropped out of sight.

G.B. GRAYSON AND IDENTITY THEFT

With his guitarist partner Henry Whitter, the blind singing fiddler Gilliam Banmon (G.B.) Grayson (1887–1930) was another influential figure of the 1920s, whose records were catalysts that revived old songs like "Tom Dooley," "Lee Highway Blues," "Ommie Wise," "Handsome Molly," and "Nine Pound Hammer," ensuring their survival and turning them into country classics. Wade and/or J.E. made good versions of Grayson's "Nobody's Darling on Earth," "Little Maggie," "Down in the Willow Garden," "Banks of the Ohio," "Don't Go Out Tonight, My Darling," and "Short Life of Trouble," informing and influencing subsequent generations that never knew him.

WADE I think it was a blind man, Grayson, and Henry Whitter who were the first I heard to play "Train 45." There was a fellow told me one time that he was Grayson. He sounded just like him, played the fiddle just like him. He come and played where we were puttin' on a show. We learned a lot from that feller, old ballads and songs. He had a good time with his fiddle; when he played you could know he was enjoying every note he hit.

Grayson's early death precluded his actually being the individual whom Wade describes. People used to claim to have seen the East Texas blues giant Blind Lemon Jefferson in far-flung places all over the south, and historians have assumed that in many if not most cases, musicians making the claim were impersonators.

The 1940s

WWNC, 1941. L to R: Jack Shelton, Tiny Dodson, Wade Mainer, Howard Dixon.

WWNC, 1941. Standing, L to R: Tiny Dodson, Marty Lyles (announcer), Howard Dixon, and Wade Mainer. Kneeling L to R: Curly Shelton, Jack Shelton.

August 20th, 1941

Mr. Wade Mainer,
Wade Mainer's "Sons Of The Mountaineers",
Station WWNC,
ASHEVILLE, NORTH CAROLINA

Dear Wade:

As you know, between July 15th and July 30th
WWNC offered to send its listeners a picture
of your organization if those listeners would
write the station requesting it. - And, brother,
they really wrote!

In 12 days you received 8,619 pieces of mail
requesting your picture. And that doesn't
include your regular fan-mail which has averaged
over 3,000 pieces a month. I think that this
response is really sensational. As a matter of
fact, the response to the picture offer has
definitely proved that your program is heard
by hundreds of thousands of people in 33 counties
located in North Carolina, South Carolina, and
Tennessee.

All in all, Wade, is just bears out the fact
that the "Sons Of The Mountaineers" is probably
the most popular hill-billy outfit we've had on
WWNC. It IS a swell outfit, - and you're entitled
to 'go places' with it!

My best wishes and a sincere 'thank you' are
certainly very much a part of this note to you.

Sincerely,

Promotion Director
STATION WWNC

Harman I. Moseley

1941 letter from WWNC to Wade.

LOOK WHO'S COMING
WADE MAINER
& HIS
SONS OF THE MOUNTAINEERS

APPEARING AT

GLENVILLE SCHOOL   **GLENVILLE, N. C.**
Thursday, Oct. 23rd   **Sponsored by the School**

FEATURING   *HEARD*
THE
ONE MAN   *DAILY*
BAND
                               OVER
PANHANDLE
PETE   *W-W-N-C*

PLAYING
INSTRUMENTS   *ASHEVILLE*
AT ONE TIME   5:30 - 6:00
                               A. M.

DON'T MISS THIS HOUR AND A HALF
OF CLEAN ENTERTAINMENT.
LOTS OF HYMN SINGING
Show Starts 7:30 P.M.

1941 poster with Panhandle Pete.

WADE He was a one man band and kind of comical with it. He carried music on his shoulders and a drum on his back. He played the mouth organ and guitar and played the cowbells on his feet. He's got a banjo-guitar there; he used several instruments like that. His name was Howard Nash and he lived in Asheville.

Wade Mainer, WWNC, 1941.

WADE I was working at WWNC in Asheville when Lowell Blanchard over at WNOX Knoxville was running the Mid-Day Merry Go Round. He came to Asheville and wanted to know if he could hire me. I said, "Sure, Lowell, I'll come down." I had a little band, I'm pretty sure it was with the Hughes brothers.

LOWELL BLANCHARD KEEPS THE MOUNTAINEERS OFF THE OPRY

One of Wade's lingering regrets is that he didn't copyright the new melody he created for Gussie L. Davis's 1880 hit "We Sat Beneath the Maple On the Hill," written when Davis was just seventeen, and recorded with Wade's own new melody in 1935. Gussie Lord Davis (1863–1899) was an African American songwriter whose list of enduring hits, including "Irene, Good Night," "In The Baggage Coach Ahead," "One Little Word," The Fatal Wedding," "Jack and May (Let Us Be Lovers Again)," and "When the Snowflakes Fall Again," would doubtlessly have continued had he lived longer. Even though sheet music for the original was still in print, Wade's popular 1935 duet with Zeke Morris consigned the original tune to permanent eclipse, and his version became an immediate hit and a country music standard.

Wade's second major regret was being denied an opportunity to work on the Grand Ole Opry in 1941. It was a larger misfortune than Wade realized at the time, and it began a series of events that marked a critical turning point in his career.

WADE I was in Knoxville just before the war broke out, and they was draftin' people. I got in trouble with Lowell Blanchard, the manager at WNOX, when the Solemn Old Judge wanted me to come and take over Pee Wee King's place on the Opry. He said, "Wade, you don't have to take an audition or anything. I'd like for you to come down and be on my program."

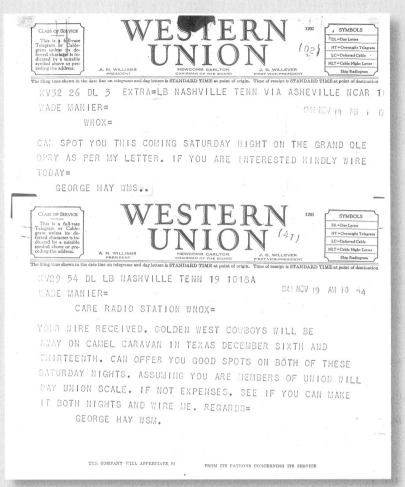

Two telegrams from George D. Hay, November 1941.

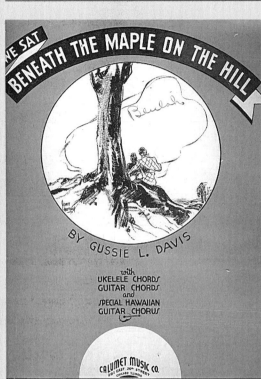

1936 sheet music for "We Sat Beneath the Maple On the Hill."

I'd signed a contract with Lowell Blanchard, so I went to him and said, "I got a chance to go on the Grand Ole Opry, what do you think?" He said, "You take it if you can get it!" He knew I was going anyhow. Well, we got it all fixed up and I had to write the judge and send him all of my numbers for ASCAP clearance.

So I worked it out with the Solemn Old Judge, but then I had to call him back and tell him I couldn't make it. Lowell Blanchard had me tied down and wouldn't let me go because mine was the only band there that they liked.

So he said, "If you leave here, you won't come back. I ain't got nobody to take your place on the Mid-Day Merry-Go-Round. If I let Wade Mainer go, I might as well close up his part of the program." So that's where I lost my job on the Opry.

I quit Lowell right off the bat. He said, "I'll fire you, I'll blackball you everywhere you go." I said, "Well go ahead and do it, I'm-a goin'." Cas Walker was waiting for me at WROL, so when I quit Cas had me on there the next morning. I didn't stay there very long.

WROL, Knoxville, late 1941 or 1942. Wade (banjo), Steve Ledford (fiddle), Hughes Brothers (guitars).

WADE That's two boys down there, lived a little ways out near where I lived that played with me some. The time was getting closer to World War II, so they got them in the Army—they had to go. My name was on the list but I escaped it. Curly and Jack Shelton had to go too.

WROL, Knoxville, late 1941 or 1942.

LIFE MAGAZINE
AND PEARL HARBOR

WADE *Life* magazine came while I was working in Knoxville. They came to the house in Asheville, took pictures there and followed me back to Knoxville. They followed me on show dates, on my broadcasts, went out through the country with me. When the war broke out, they closed everything down—they got it, but they ain't put it out yet!

Life prepared a feature on Wade, J.E., the Carter Family, and Bascom Lamar Lunsford for the issue that was abruptly altered after the United States entered World War II on December 7, 1941. The article never appeared, and the accompanying photos are not readily accessible.

Wade at WBBO, sorting mail, 1943 or 1950.

WADE That was down there in Forest City, North Carolina. It was only a hundred watt station. I passed by there one day and went in to talk to the manager. He had heard about me. He said, "I got a sponsor if you want to work," and I said, "Yeah, I'll take the job." It was Acme Tractors—yard tractors, mowing machines. True Pack Aspirin was another sponsor.

JULIA That might've been around 1950, when we lived in Woodfin and Elk Mountain.

WADE That's where Jim and Jesse played with me a while. I went over in Virginia and got 'em. I told 'em, I said, "You boys are too good to play with me and I can't afford to pay you. Get you a good band together and stick it out and do your own thing." They went on their own.

1943 festival poster.

WADE We were living in Asheville at that time. I talked to the town [Rutherford] and told them I thought the festival would be good. I had some dancers, cloggers, come over from Canton. It didn't last long. I put this Sundown festival on for 'em and run it two times, but that's when that polio disease hit. People in town were so nice, they came out, spent money and built up the festival there in the ball park, and then they said we couldn't go on with it.

Polly and Leon Mainer, born 1944.

Death Takes Mainer, 97, In Hospital

W. Joe Mainer, 97, of Weaverville died in a hospital here this morning at 7:30 o'clock. He was a life-long resident of Buncombe county.

Mr. Mainer came to Weaverville as an infant from Madison county where he was born May 13, 1850.

Funeral services will be conducted tomorrow at 3 o'clock in Union Chapel Baptist church of which he was a member and chairman of the board of deacons.

Survivors include five sons, Wade of Weaverville, Finley and James of Marion, J. E., of Concord, and Willis of Asheville; two daughters, Mrs. Essie Banks and Mrs. Eva Coates of Weaverville; 49 grandchildren and a number of great grandchildren.

West funeral home, Weaverville is in charge of arrangements, which are incomplete.

W.J. Mainer obituary, August 16, 1947.

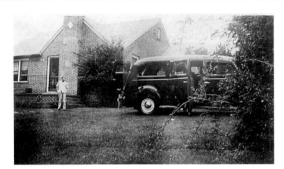

Hearse in driveway of Wade and Julia Mainer's Stony Knob home.

W.J. and Polly Mainer burial site, near Weaverville, N.C.

WADE My dad was a big healthy fellow, never sick a day in his life. He lived to be 97. He was living with us in Stony Knob when he died from a little infection in his arm and it turned into something like gangrene. Back then they didn't have the medicine to doctor with like they do now, and so they had to take his left shoulder and arm off. I think that he just gave up and that's what killed him. He was a fine Christian man.

Campaigning with Gov. Kerr Scott, Statesville, 1948. Scott was governor
from 1949–53 and U.S. senator from 1954–58.

WADE They invited us to Statesville for a big dinner. They brought big
steaks out there; we got to eatin' on 'em and somebody said, "That's all
horse meat!" Turned out it was. It didn't taste different to me, so I ate it.

Men do not quit playing because they grow old; they grow old because they quit playing.

—Oliver Wendell Holmes

WADE I left the music field and came to Michigan in 1953. I applied for and accepted a job at General Motors and retired in 1972. After that we started to play concerts; Julia and I accepted bookings that took us to the East Coast, West Coast, Canada, Holland, and Italy.

In 1987 we went down to Washington to get the National Heritage Award. We had a wonderful time. Everything went over nicely and people seemed to think a whole lot of the old time music. I was glad to get it and glad to play a few songs.

In 2002 Julia and I appeared on the Grand Ole Opry with our friend and bass player Virgil Shouse. I was also Grand Marshal for the Uncle Dave Macon Days in Murfreesboro, Tennessee in 2002.

With Minnie Pearl at Fan Fair, Nashville, Tennessee, 14 June 1975.

Nashville's Country Music Association created the Fan Fair in 1972 as an annual event for performers and personalities both to entertain on stage and mingle with fans in informal settings. More formally, it's the Country Music Association (CMA) Music Festival.

WADE They started a Fan Fair for the old people 'way back there years ago. They got it going pretty good, and we had it for three years or four; it was for the old retired musicians. The young people there wanted to push the old people out, and they took over. Sold pictures, records and all, that's what they wanted it for.

JULIA We went down to Nashville for the WSM Fan Fair two or three times in the seventies.

WADE I'll never forget this fellow that ran the dance team, I forget his name. He wanted me to play and let his band back me up. I said I don't know if they'd know my music. He said they could play any kind of music you want. We rehearsed a little and I said I wanted them to lead it out. I said I wanted my wife with me, but they wouldn't let her be with me; she had to stand 'way over in a corner. We got on stage and waited for the signal light. But when the light shone, nobody played. I looked around at the band but they couldn't do it, couldn't kick it off. I told that fellow, "Don't you ever bring that band around me any more!"

Leon Mainer (deceased) was Polly's twin brother and was
musically active. He served in Viet Nam with the US Army
Reserves and made 2nd Lieutenant before being honorably
discharged in 1976.

Berea College, October 1979.

Zeke Morris and Wade, Cliffside, North Carolina, 1980.

The Southwest Folklore Center & The School of Music

University of Arizona

presents

OLD TIME MOUNTAIN MUSIC

featuring

WADE & JULIA MAINER

and introducing

"MR. BILL" HENSLEY

| February 17, 1982 | Crowder Hall |
| Wednesday, 8:00 P.M. | Univ. of Arizona |

No Admission Charge. Opportunity will be given for donations. For information call 626-3392.

1982 poster for University of Arizona appearance.

Arizona photos

WADE We used to go out there on vacations. Jim Griffith had something to do with it. It was at the university. He was a professor and got us down there. Then two or three boys wanted us to come up to Flagstaff and we went. We took a motor home and went out in the desert with the sand and scorpions and snakes. We stayed in that motor home.

JULIA That was on BLM [Bureau of Land Management] land.

WADE You could set up out there and it wouldn't cost you nothing; it was government land, taxpayers' land.

The government went out there and put up some water so people from the north could come out there and spend the winter, you know. Then people got to being so rude and bad, dumping trash out on the desert, and they stopped it.

JULIA We went out there for a number of years and didn't go back after our house burned down in 1997.

Julia, Wade, and Randall, early 1980s.

Wade with his banjo trick did this - on most of personal appearances - Randy (son) on guitar - Wade & Julia

10th International Folk Music Festival

Florence Italy Nov 2,3 - 1986

10th International Folk Music Festival, Florence, Italy,
2–3 November 1986.

Wade displaying comic abilities, with Randall and Julia, 1980s.

WADE They went wild over our singing. When we wound up
our show they came out and wrapped Julia up in flowers.

Poster from European tour, August 1983.

JULIA That was a wonderful time, first time we'd ever been overseas. A.G. & Kate met us in Brussels and took us to their home, which was several hours away in Rijn [Ryen], Holland. We had a day of rest and then we started on the tour that lasted a couple of weeks. They took us almost to the North Sea.

SMITHSONIAN INSTITUTION

WASHINGTON, D. C. 20560

Office of Folklife Programs
January 21, 1982

Mr. Wade Mainer
c/o Jim Griffith
Southwestern Lore Center
University of Arizona
1524 Gamma Apts.
Tucson, Arizona 85715

Dear Mr. Mainer:

We are very pleased that you will be joining us on the
evening of Sunday, January 31st to celebrate the 100th
anniversary of the birth of Franklin Delano Roosevelt. It
promises to be an exciting event, and your participation
will help to make it something we can all be proud of.

The celebration will be held in the Pendulum Hall of
the National Musuem of American History. We have reserved
the space on Saturday evening from 7:00 until 10:00 pm for a
rehearsal of Sunday night's performance. Please plan to have
eaten by 6:30 so that you can be on time to board the bus.
We have scheduled the bus to pick you up at 6:45 at the Park
Central Hotel where most of you will be staying. If you will
not be able to attend the rehearsal, please let me know so
that we can make alternate arrangements for discussing your
role in the evening with you.

We have reserved a plane ticket for your trip to
Washington. You are scheduled to leave Tucson at 9:30 am on
Friday January 29th. Your plane is Eastern # 712, arriving
at Washington National at 6:31 pm. Your return plane departs
from Washington National on Monday, February 1st at 8:04 am,
arriving at Tucson at 1:32 pm. Your tickets, as well as an
itinerary will be mailed to you ahead of time. Please
arrange to be at Tucson one hour before departure time in
order to have plenty of time to locate and board your plane.
Upon arrival in Washington, take local transportation to the
Park Central Hotel at 705 18th St. N.W. We have made
reservations in your name at the hotel.

The hotel is fairly close to the museum where you will
be performing. We presently have reserved a double room for
you to share with Julia for the weekend. They have given us
a special rate of $42.00 for a single room and $48.00 for a
double. You will be responsible for paying the cost of your
room upon your departure. If we have reserved a single room

--2--

for you and you would like us to attempt to put you in a
room with another participant instead, notify me immediately
and we will make every attempt to do so.

To help offset your food and lodging expenses while you
are here, we will give you a check for $225.00 on the
evening of the concert. In addition we will include the
amount of $300.00 as a token of our appreciation for your
participation. Since banks will be closed over the weekend,
please bring enough money to cover your hotel bill and other
expenses while you are here. If this presents a problem,
please let us know.

We require that you sign a release, a copy of which is
enclosed with this letter. Basically, the release says that
we can use films, photos, videotapes, etc. of your
performance for non-profit, educational uses. Any use for
profit requires your further permission. Please read the
release carefully, and contact me if you have any questions.
You will be required to sign the release prior to receiving
your check.

I have enclosed a copy of the recent brochure
describing the events to be held in Washington to celebrate
the Roosevelt Centennary. As you can see, we are one of many
events being planned to honor this very special man.

If you have any questions about your participation or
the arrangements we made for you, please call me person
-to-person, collect at (202) 287-3436. It has been a
pleasure corresponding with you and I am looking forward to
our meeting in Washington. Our event will be free and open
to the public. We want to share your talents with all who
can attend.

Warm Regards,

Diana Parker

Diana Parker
Program Coordinator

1982 Smithsonian letter for FDR
100th anniversary concert.

With author (L), Delaware Valley Bluegrass Festival, 1980s.

L to R: Virgil Shouse, Wade, Frank, Julia, and Randall Mainer. WFBE, Flint, where Frank worked from 1980 to 1990.

Jim (L) and Jesse McReynolds played some of their earliest engagements with Wade, around 1950.

With Charles Whitstein of the Whitstein Brothers, 1980s.

NATIONAL
ENDOWMENT
FOR
THE ARTS

WASHINGTON
D.C. 20506

A Federal agency advised by the
National Council on the Arts

National Heritage Award 1987

National Heritage Award 1987

Mr. Wade Mainer
1408 West Hill Road
Flint, MI 48507

1 0 SEP 1987

Dear Mr. Mainer:

It is my pleasure to notify you that you have been awarded a
National Heritage Fellowship Award of $5,000 from the Folk Arts
Program of the National Endowment for the Arts for the purpose
of helping you to pursue your artistic career. The identifying
number for this grant is 87-5532-0126.

The Endowment is pleased to honor you in this way and to pay
tribute to your many contributions to the field of folk arts.

Sincerely,

F. S. M. HODSOLL
Chairman

Reference:
Application Number: A87-013178

Enclosures:
1. Folk Arts Heritage Fellowship Grant
   Acceptance Instructions and Agreement

THE WHITE HOUSE

WASHINGTON

Santa Barbara

August 25, 1987

Dear Mr. Mainer:

I am happy to congratulate you as the National Endowment
for the Arts awards you a National Heritage Fellowship.

Your unique talents and achievements are a source of pride
and enrichment for our Nation. Our land has been blessed
with a rich tapestry of cultural and artistic traditions,
and your work represents one of the finest examples of this
richness. Your dedication to developing and sharing your
God-given talents is a shining example of the spirit that has
made America great.

Nancy and I want you to know how proud we are of your
achievements, and we wish you every success and happiness
in the years to come. God bless you.

Sincerely,

Ronald Reagan

Mr. Wade Mainer
1408 West Hill Road
Flint, Michigan 48507

The Folk Arts Program
of the National Endowment
for the Arts recognizes

Wade Mainer

s a Master Traditional Artist
who has contributed to
the shaping of our artistic
traditions and to preserving
the cultural diversity of
the United States

Chairman, National Endowment for the Arts

Director, Folk Arts Program

CARL LEVIN
MICHIGAN

United States Senate
WASHINGTON, DC 20510

August 7, 1987

Mr. Wade Mainer
1408 W. Hill Road
Flint, Michigan 48507

Dear Mr. Mainer:

I wish to congratulate you upon being a
National Endowment for the Arts award recipient
as exemplary master folk artist.

Noting that your specialty is banjo, you
might wish to go to the Arena Stage Vat Room
for a performance of "Banjo Dancing" when you
are here in October. Steven Wade is now in his
7th year there.

And of course you are welcome to drop by
my office to say hello if your schedule allows,
but please call in advance. Once again,
congratulations.

Sincerely,

Carl Levin

CL/hgp
cc: Frank Hodsoll

With award and U.S. Rep. Dale E. Kildee (D, 5th District, Michigan).

L to R: Alan Lomax, Wade, Bess Lomax Hawes.

Banjo Meltdown, Lebanon, TN, 1990. L to R: John Hartford, Wade, unknown.

Banjo Meltdown, Lebanon, TN, 1990. L to R: Wade, Ramona Jones, Grandpa Jones, Julia.

Wade at home on West Hill Road in Flint.

Wade and Julia in front of their home in Flint, just after it was destroyed in a 1997 fire.

Randall, Wade, and Polly outside Wade and Julia's current home in Flint.

Trophies and awards in the Mainer home before the fire.

Burned awards, Mainers' front porch, 2007.

Uncle Dave Macon Days Heritage Award, 13 July 2002.

With Mike Seeger, ca. 2000.

With Bill Carlisle backstage at Grand Ole Opry, 12 July 2002.

With Sonny Osborne backstage at the Opry.

With Little Jimmy Dickens backstage at the Opry.

With Eddie Stubbs (L) and Little Jimmy Dickens backstage at the Opry.

Wade and Julia with Bill Anderson and Eddie Stubbs (R) backstage at the Opry.

Christmas 2006 at the home of Polly Mainer Hofmeister and Ralph Frederick, Rochester Hills, Michigan. Standing L to R: Andrea Hofmeister, Carma Mainer, Wade Mainer, Todd Hofmeister, Julia Mae Brown Mainer, Polly Mainer Hofmeister, Randall Mainer. Seated, L to R: Stephen Hoffmann, Melina Chase Hoffmann, Stacy Hoffmann.

Julia, Melina, Wade, Mainers' living room, recent.

L to R: Ralph Frederick, Polly Mainer Hofmeister, Eva Mainer, Frank Mainer, Carma Mainer, Randall Mainer, Julia Mainer, Wade Mainer, Kelly Mainer.

L to R: Polly, Wade, Julia, Kelly, Frank, and Randall, recent.

UNITED STATES SENATOR
WASHINGTON, D.C. 20510

DEBBIE STABENOW
MICHIGAN

April 21, 2007

Wade Mainer
G3327 Herrick St
Flint, MI 48532

Best wishes . . .

. . . on the occasion of your 100th birthday.

I join your family and friends in wishing you all the best as you
celebrate this exciting day. You have reached an amazing milestone!!
I know your wisdom and experience have benefited those who have
the privilege of knowing you.

Again, congratulations and best wishes for a wonderful birthday.

Sincerely,

Debbie Stabenow
United States Senator

DS:hf

  NOT PRINTED AT GOVERNMENT EXPENSE

Wade Mainer Turns 100

The author, Julia, and Wade, Mainers' front
yard, October 2007.

April 21, 2007

Mr. Wade Mainer
c/o Ralph L. Frederick
1817 Apple Ridge Court
Rochester Hills, MI 48306

Dear Mr. Mainer:

On behalf of Officers and Trustees and the staff of the Country Music Hall of Fame® and Museum, I would like to join your family and friends in extending heartfelt congratulations as you mark your centennial birthday. Being able to recognize, on such an auspicious occasion, the many contributions you have made to music over the past 70 years is one of the privileges of my position. Paying tribute to those of you who paved the way for the success of others is an honor I treasure.

That rich musical soil of Western North Carolina and East Tennessee must have been fertile indeed to produce stellar pioneers such as you and your brother J.E., Doc Watson, Wiley and Zeke Morris, Clyde Moody, Chet Atkins, Roy Acuff, and others. The term "proto-bluegrass" is one with which I doubt many today are familiar, but as an architect of that style, characterized by your unique two-finger style of banjo picking, you most certainly were a stand-out among your peers. I am delighted to tell you that your contributions to the rise of string bands is immortalized in the Museum's recently-published book, *Will the Circle Be Unbroken: Country Music in America,* on page 80. How fascinating it must have been to play at Franklin Roosevelt's White House!

Mr. Mainer, please be assured that those of us who devote ourselves each day to preserving the roots and heritage of our music salute you on this landmark event. Happy birthday and congratulations on your long and illustrious career. We are very grateful for your endeavors in breaking new musical ground and nurturing traditions that continue to influence country music.

Warm regards,

Kyle Young
Director

The Country Music Hall of Fame® and Museum is operated by the Country Music Foundation, Inc.®, a Section 501(c)(3) not-for-profit educational organization chartered by the state of Tennessee in 1964.

222 FIFTH AVENUE SOUTH | NASHVILLE, TN 37203 | PHONE 615.416.2001 | FAX 615.255.2245
www.countrymusichalloffame.com

Broadcast Chronology

Early country music groups and southern radio stations mutually profited from their interdependence. The stations, their sponsors, and listeners enjoyed inexpensive live entertainment, while musicians profited from the high profile they received in return, allowing them to attract sponsors, sell records and souvenir songbooks, and draw audiences to personal appearances. The downside of this arrangement was that they could perform only for limited periods of time, usually a few months, until the area was "played out" and they had to move to another station and new market where their appeal was fresh once more.

This is a list of the stations that Wade remembers, where Mainers' Mountaineers worked until 1937, and where Wade's own groups appeared afterwards.

WSOC Gastonia (The Wayside Station)	1933–34
WBT Charlotte (Crazy Barn Dance)	1934–35
WWL New Orleans	1935
WWNC (*Wonderful Western North Carolina*) Asheville	1935
WSJS Winston-Salem	1935
WSJS Winston-Salem (Julia)	1935–37
WPTF Raleigh	1935–37
WBT Charlotte	1937
WIS Columbia, SC	1938
WPTF Raleigh	1939
WAIR Winston-Salem	1940
WWNC Asheville	1941
W??? Danville, VA	1941
WNOX, WROL Knoxville	1941–early 1942

WBBO Forest City, NC	1943 (as soloist);
	ca. 1950
	(with Jim & Jesse)
WGST(?) Atlanta	1944
WWNC Asheville	mid-1940s

FIRST RECORDS

Wade, J.E., and the Mountaineers were invited to make records for RCA's Bluebird label in 1935. Recording director Eli Oberstein had a particular need for a good string band at the moment. Milton Brown's Musical Brownies, a popular western swing outfit, had left the label at the end of 1934, and began to sell a lot of records for the rival Decca label in 1935. Bluebird was still recording Bill Boyd's Cowboy Ramblers in Texas, but Oberstein correctly felt that his label needed comparable talent from the Southeast. The Mainers traveled to a field recording session at the Winecoff Hotel in Atlanta. On August 6, 1935, they recorded several best-sellers, including "This World Is Not My Home," "New Curly Headed Baby," "Lights in the Valley," and "Maple On the Hill," Wade's enduring arrangement of a popular song from 1880.

WADE When we got with a record company and got some records out, people began to like us a lot better. They didn't play records on the station back then, I mean the RCA records. We were there live at WPTF till our records come out. Then they began to play our records and we could slow up a little bit, get a little rest, get a little sleep.

Discography

This chapter documents all known published recordings by Wade Mainer and includes all available information about each session. All early titles from 1935 through matrix BS 011823 (2 August 1937) appear on the boxed compact disc set *J.E. Mainer[,] The Early Years*, JSP Records JSP77118, and a forthcoming set that will contain remaining pre–World War II performances. Sessions by J.E. Mainer's Mountaineers without Wade are omitted here; solo performances by others without Wade are included when they constitute part of a Wade Mainer session.

All titles made through 1953 originally appeared as 78 rpm 10" discs. Some 1951 King couplings may have appeared as both 78 and 45 rpm singles. Montgomery Ward issues through M-7480 are credited to Mainer's Mountaineers. Montgomery Ward also applied the credit to performances by (and credited to) J.E. Mainer on Bluebird, whether or not they included Wade. Composer credits appear on post–World War II records only.

Releases indicated in italics are 33 1/3 or 45 rpm pressings or compact discs (CD). All releases after 1953 are in one or another of these formats; 45 rpm discs and CDs are noted; all others are 33 1/3.

These labels are cited, some with abbreviations:

AL [Audio Lab] (33)
Bb [Bluebird] (78)
Blue Ridge (78)
County (33, CD)
Dust-to-Digital (CD)
Gusto (CD)
IRMA (33)
June Appal (CD)
King (78, 33, 45)
Knob (45)

MW [Montgomery Ward] (78)
OH [Old Homestead] (33, CD)
RCA [RCA Victor] (all formats)
Revenant (CD)
RZ [Regal Zonophone] (78)
    G series: Australia
    MR series: England
Twin (India, 78)
Vi [Victor] (78)
Yazoo (CD)

J.E. MAINER'S MOUNTAINEERS

BS 94328-1	Ship Sailing Now	Bb B-6088, MW M-4714, *OH OHCD-4013 (CD)*
BS 94329-1	This World Is Not My Home [*Zeke Morris solo*]	Bb B-6088, MW M-4714
BS 94330-1	Maple On the Hill	Bb B-6065, MW M-4969, RCA 20-3241, DJ606, *8416-2 (CD)*, RZ G22837
BS 94331-1	Take Me In the Lifeboat	Bb B-6065, MW M-4969, RZ G22837

Wade Mainer-vocal, banjo; Zeke Morris-tenor vocal, guitar
Winecoff Hotel, Atlanta, 6 August 1935

Regal Zonophone G22837 as MELODY MOUNTAINEERS

BS 94332-1	Seven and a Half (1)	Bb B-6792, MW M-7009, *8416-2 (CD)*
BS 94333-1	New Curly Headed Baby (2,3)	Bb B-6104, MW M-4970
BS 94338-1	Let Her Go, God Bless Her (1,3,4)	Bb B-6104, MW M-4970
BS 94339-1	City On the Hill (1,2,3,4)	Bb B-6160, MW M-4711, *OH 194 (33), OHCD-4013 (CD)*

BS 94340-1	The Longest Train (1,3,4)	Bb B-6222, MW M-7005
BS 94341-1	Write a Letter to Mother (2,3,4)	Bb B-6194, MW M-4716
BS 94342-1	Lights In the Valley (1,2,3,4)	Bb B-6160, MW M-4711, RCA 20-3241, *OH 194 (33)*, *OHCD-4013 (CD)*

J.E. Mainer-fiddle, (1)vocal; Wade Mainer-banjo, (2)vocal; Zeke Morris-guitar, (3)vocal; Daddy John Love-guitar, (4)vocal
Winecoff Hotel, Atlanta, 6 August 1935

WADE MAINER-ZEKE MORRIS

BS 99133-1	Come Back To Your Dobie Shack (1)	Bb B-6551, MW M-4719
BS 99134-1	Just As the Sun Went Down [*Zeke Morris solo*]	Bb B-6383, MW M-4718
BS 99135-1	What Would You Give In Exchange	Bb B-8073, MW M-7134, *OH OHCD-4013 (CD)*
BS 99136-1	A Leaf From the Sea (1)	Bb B-6347, MW M-4713
BS 99137-1	Brown Eyes	Bb B-6347, MW M-4713

Wade Mainer-vocal, banjo, (1)harmonica; Zeke Morris-tenor vocal, guitar
Charlotte, 14 February 1936

BS 99138-1	Maple On the Hill—Part 2 (Drifting To That Happy Home)	Bb B-6293, MW M-4710
BS 99139-1	Going To Georgia (1)	Bb B-6423, MW M-4719
BS 99140-1	Nobody's Darling But Mine	Bb B-6423

| BS 99141-1 | Mother Came To Get Her Boy From Jail | Bb B-6383, MW M-4718, *OH OHCD-4013 (CD)* |
| BS 99142-1 | Where the Red, Red Roses Grow (1) | Bb B-6293, MW M-4718, Twin FT8094 |

Wade Mainer-vocal, banjo, (1)harmonica; Zeke Morris-tenor vocal, guitar
Charlotte, 15 February 1936

J.E. MAINER'S MOUNTAINEERS

BS 102600-1	On a Cold Winter Night (2)	Bb B-6629, MW M-7008, Vi 27496
BS 102601-1	John Henry Was a Little Boy (1,2,3)	Bb B-6629, MW M-7008, *Revenant 211(CD)*
BS 102602-1	The Old and Faded Picture (1,2,3)	Bb B-6479, MW M-5035, *OH OHCD-4013 (CD)*
BS 102603-1	Take Me Home To the Sweet Sunny South (2)	Bb B-6479, MW M-5035, *OH OHCD-4013 (CD)*
BS 102604-1	Walk That Lonesome Valley (1,2,3)	Bb B-6456, MW M-7007, *OH 194 (33), OHCD-4013 (CD)*
BS 102605-1	Got a Home In That Rock (1,2,3)	Bb B-6456, MW M-7007, *OH 194 (33), OHCD-4013 (CD)*
BS 102606-1	Johnson's Old Grey Mule (1,2)	Bb B-6584, MW M-7006, *RCA 8416-2 (CD)*
BS 102607-1	Won't Be Worried Long (1,2,3)	Bb B-6738, MW M-7009
BS 102608-1	Goin' Down the River Of Jordan (1,2,3)	Bb B-6539, MW M-7004, *OHCD-4013 (CD)*
BS 102609-1	Why Do You Bob Your Hair, Girls? (1)	Bb B-6792, MW M-7131
BS 102610-1	Down Among the Budded Roses (1)	Bb unissued

| BS 102611-1 | Watermelon On the Vine (1,2,3,4) | Bb B-6584, MW M-7006 |

J.E. Mainer-fiddle, (1)vocal; Wade Mainer-banjo, (2)vocal; Zeke Morris-guitar, (3)vocal; Beacham Blackweller-guitar, (4)vocal
Charlotte, 15 June 1936

Junior Misenhimer (banjo) and Harold Christy (guitar) have been credited with participating in this session; nevertheless, Wade Mainer confirms that he is the only banjo player present.

WADE MAINER–ZEKE MORRIS

BS 102612-1	Cradle Days (1)	Bb B-6489, MW M-5031
BS 102613-1	Gathering Flowers From the Hills	Bb B-6489, MW M-5031
BS 102614-1	My Mother Is Waiting	Bb B-6653, MW M-7091, *OH OHCD-4013 (CD)*
BS 102615-1	If I Could Hear My Mother	Bb B-6653, MW M-7091
	If I Could Hear My Mother Pray Again	*OH OHCD-4013 (CD)*
BS 102616-1	Nobody's Darling On Earth	Bb B-6653, MW M-7091
BS 102617-1	Shake Hands With Mother	Bb B-6653, MW M-7091
	Shake Hands With Mother Again	*OH OHCD-4013 (CD)*

Wade Mainer–vocal, banjo; Zeke Morris–tenor vocal, guitar; (1)Norwood Tew–vocal
Charlotte, 15 June 1936

MAINER'S MOUNTAINEERS

BS 102622-1	I Miss My Mother and Dad	MW M-7133
BS 102623-1	They Said My Lord Was a Devil	Rejected

Zeke Morris–vocal, guitar; George Morris–vocal and guitar
Charlotte, 15 June 1936

Wade Mainer did not participate on these recordings; his next recording recycled the second title.

WADE MAINER–ZEKE MORRIS

BS 02530-1	They Said My Lord Was a Devil	Bb B-6653, MW M-7091, *OH 194 (33), OHCD-4013 (CD)*
BS 02531-1	Won't Somebody Pal With Me (1)	Bb B-6704, MW M-7092
BS 02532-1	Hop Along Peter (1)	Bb B-6752, MW M-7131
BS 02533-1	Just One Way To the Pearly Gates (1)	Bb B-6784, MW M-7132
BS 02534-1	Dear Daddy You're Gone	Bb B-6752, MW M-7133, RZ G23374, *OH OHCD-4013 (CD)*
BS 02535-1	Been Foolin' Me, Baby (1)	Bb B-6704, MW M-7092
BS 02536-1	I'll Be a Friend of Jesus (1)	Bb B-6784, MW M-7132, *Dust-to-Digital 01 (CD)*
BS 02537-1	Cowboy's Pony in Heaven	Bb B-6653, MW M-7091
BS 02548-1	The Good Southern Soda (1)	*OH OHCS-5124 (33)*

Wade Mainer–vocal, banjo; Zeke Morris–tenor vocal, guitar; Homer "Pappy" Sherrill–fiddle, (1)vocal
Charlotte, 12 October 1936

Bluebird labels credit **Wade Mainer–Zeke Morris–Homer Sherrill** on titles where the latter's voice is heard. BS 02548 was a privately pressed commercial for Old Sam's Soda, and has been issued only on Old Homestead. Montgomery Ward labels as usual credit only **Mainer's Mountaineers**.

BS 07051-1	Little Birdie (2)	Bb B-6840, MW M-7127
BS 07052-1	Always Been a Rambler	Bb B-6890, MW M-7129
BS 07053-1	Starting Life Anew With You (2)	Bb B-6840, MW M-7130
BS 07054-1	Little Rosebuds (2)	Bb B-6993, MW M-7127, Twin FT8419, *OH OHCD-4013 (CD)*
BS 07055-1	Train Carry My Girl Back Home (1) [*Wade Mainer solo*]	Bb B-6890, MW M-7129
BS 07056-1	In the Land Beyond the Blue [*Zeke Morris solo*]	Bb B-6936, MW M-7128
BS 07057-1	A Change All Around (2)	Bb B-6993, MW M-7130, Twin FT8419
BS 07058-1	Short Life and It's Trouble (2)	Bb B-6936, MW M-7128, *RCA 8416-2 (CD)*

Wade Mainer–vocal, banjo or (1)guitar; Zeke Morris–guitar, (2)tenor vocal
Charlotte, 16 February 1937

BS 011812-1	Dying Boy's Prayer	Bb B-7165, MW M-7306, *OH OHCD-4013 (CD)*
BS 011813-1	Free Again	Bb B-7114, MW M-7306, Twin FT8492
BS 011814-1	Answer to "Two Little Rosebuds"	Bb B-7114, MW M-7307, Twin FT8492
BS 011815-1	I'm Not Turning Backward	Bb B-7165, MW M-7308, *OH OHCD-4013 (CD)*

Wade Mainer–vocal, banjo; Zeke Morris–tenor vocal, guitar
Charlotte, 2 August 1937

WADE MAINER–ZEKE MORRIS–STEVE LEDFORD

| BS 011820-1 | Riding On That Train Forty-Five | Bb B-7298, Vi 27493 |
| BS 011821-1 | Little Maggie (1) | Bb B-7201, MW M-7309 |

Wade Mainer–banjo; Zeke Morris–guitar, (1)tenor vocal; Steve Ledford–lead vocal, fiddle
Charlotte, 2 August 1937

WADE MAINER–ZEKE MORRIS

| BS 011822-1 | Little Pal (1) | Bb B-7201, MW M-7309 |
| BS 011823-1 | Down In the Willow | Bb B-7298, MW M-7307, Vi 27497 |

Wade Mainer–vocal, banjo; Zeke Morris–guitar, (1)tenor vocal; Steve Ledford–fiddle
Charlotte, 2 August 1937

WADE MAINER AND HIS LITTLE SMILIN' RANGERS

BS 011825-1	Ramshackle Shack (1,2,3)	Bb B-7274, MW M-7310
BS 011826-1	Memory Lane (3)	Bb B-7274, MW M-7310, RZ MR2687, Twin FT8504
BS 011827-1	Wild Bill Jones	Bb B-7249, MW M-7311
BS 011828-1	I Want To Be Loved (2)	Bb B-7249, MW M-7311

Wade Mainer–vocal, banjo, (1)harmonica; (2)Morris (Buddy) Banks–vocal; (3) Robert (Buck) Banks–steel guitar; Zeke Morris–guitar
Charlotte, 2 August 1937

| BS 011816-1 | What Are You Going To Do, Brother? | Bb B-7384 |
| BS 011817-1 | Companions Draw Nigh | Bb B-7384 |

BS 011818-1	Mountain Sweetheart	Bb B-7587
BS 011819-1	Don't Forget Me, Little Darling	Bb B-7587

Morris (Buddy) Banks–vocal, mandolin; Robert (Buck) Banks–vocal, guitar
Charlotte, 3 August 1937

WADE MAINER AND SONS OF THE MOUNTAINEERS

BS 018763-1	Lonely Tomb (1)	Bb B-7424, MW M-7480
BS 018764-1	Pale Moonlight (1)	Bb B-7483, MW M-7481
BS 018765-1	All My Friends	Bb B-7424, MW M-7480
BS 018767-1	Don't Get Too Deep In Love	Bb B-7483, MW M-7481
BS 018768-1	Don't Leave Me Alone (1)	Bb B-7561, MW M-7482
BS 018769-1	I Won't Be Worried (1)	Bb B-7561, MW M-7482
BS 018772-1	Mitchell Blues (no vocal)	Bb B-7845, MW M-7484

Wade Mainer–vocal, banjo; Steve Ledford–fiddle, (1)tenor vocal; Clyde
Moody–guitar; Jay Hugh Hall–guitar
Charlotte, 27 January 1938

BS 018767 is a song known as "A Dark Road Is a Hard Road to Travel," first
recorded by G. B. Grayson and Henry Whitter in 1929. "Don't Get Too Deep
In Love" was recorded as "I Met Her At a Ball One Night" (BS 032628) on 4
February 1939.

BS 018770-1	Where Romance Calls	Bb B-7753, MW-M-7483

Julia Mae Mainer–vocal, guitar; Steve Ledford–fiddle
Charlotte, 27 January 1938

| BS 018771-1 | Another Alabama Camp Meetin' | Bb B-7753, MW M-7484 |

Wade Mainer–vocal, banjo
Charlotte, 27 January 1938

STEVE LEDFORD AND THE MOUNTAINEERS

BS 018766-1	Since I Met My Mother-In-Law	Bb B-7742, MW M-7483
BS 018779-1	Bachelor Blues	Bb B-7626
BS 018780-1	Only a Broken Heart (1)	Bb B-7626
BS 018781-1	Happy Or Lonesome (1)	Bb B-7742

Steve Ledford–vocal, fiddle; Jay Hugh Hall–guitar, (1)tenor vocal; Clyde Moody–guitar, (1)harmony vocal; Wade Mainer–banjo
Charlotte, 27 January 1938

WADE MAINER AND SONS OF THE MOUNTAINEERS

| BS 026981-1 | Farther Along (1) | Bb B-8023, MW M-7560 |
| BS 026982-1 | Dear Loving Mother and Dad | Bb B-8152, MW M-7561 |

Clyde Moody–lead vocal, harmony vocal on chorus, guitar; Wade Mainer–lead vocal on chorus; Steve Ledford–fiddle; Jay Hugh Hall–guitar
Rock Hill, SC, 26 September 1938

| BS 026983-1 | Can't Tell About These Women | Bb B-7965, MW M-7562 |

Clyde Moody–lead vocal, guitar; Jay Hugh Hall–tenor vocal, guitar; Steve Ledford–fiddle, Wade Mainer–banjo
Rock Hill, SC, 26 September 1938

BS 026984-1	That Kind	Bb B-7861, MW M-7562
BS 026998-1	You're Awfully Mean To Me	Bb B-7861, MW M-7565
BS 026999-1	Home in the Sky	Bb B-8007, MW M-7560, Twin FT8716
BS 027700-1	A Little Love	Bb B-7924, MW M-7563
BS 027701-1	North Carolina Moon	Bb B-8628, MW M-7564

Clyde Moody–lead vocal, guitar; Jay Hugh Hall–tenor vocal, guitar
Rock Hill, SC, 26 September 1938

Bluebird B-7924 as **Wade Mainer and his Blue Ridge Buddies**

BS 026985-1	If I Had Listened To Mother	Bb B-8137, MW M-7561
BS 026987-1	The Same Old You To Me (1)	Bb B-7924, MW M-7564
BS 026997-1	Mother Still Prays For You Jack (1)	Bb B-8137, MW M-7563
BS 027702-1	More Good Women Gone Wrong (1)	Bb B-7965, MW M-7565

Steve Ledford–lead vocal, fiddle; Jay Hugh Hall–tenor vocal; Wade Mainer–banjo; Clyde Moody–guitar, (1)harmony vocal
Rock Hill, SC, 26 September 1938

Bluebird B-7924 as **Wade Mainer and his Blue Ridge Buddies**

BS 026986-1	She Is Spreading Her Wings For a Journey	Bb B-8023, MW M-7559
BS 026988-1	Life's Ev'nin' Sun	Bb B-8007, MW M-7559, Twin FT8716

Wade Mainer–vocal, banjo; Jay Hugh Hall–guitar, tenor vocal; Clyde Moody–harmony vocal, guitar
Rock Hill, SC, 26 September 1938

BS 032625-1	Sparkling Blue Eyes	Bb B-8042, MW M-7882, RCA 20-2159
BS 032626-1	We Will Miss Him	Bb B-8042, MW M-7882
BS 032631-1	One Little Kiss	Bb B-8145
BS 032632-1	Mama Don't Make Me Go To Bed (1)	Bb B-8145

Clyde Moody–lead vocal, guitar; Jay Hugh Hall–tenor vocal, guitar; (1)Wade Mainer–banjo
Rock Hill, SC, 4 February 1939

BS 032627-1	I Left My Home In the Mountains	Bb B-8091, MW M-7883
BS 032628-1	I Met Her At a Ball One Night (1)	Bb B-8091, MW M-7883
BS 032629-1	You May Forsake Me	Bb B-8120, *County 404 (33)*
BS 032633-1	Crying Holy	Bb B-8203
BS 032634-1	Heaven Bells Are Ringing	Bb B-8203, *OH OHCD-4013 (CD)*

Wade Mainer–vocal, banjo; Jay Hugh Hall–tenor vocal, guitar; Clyde Moody–harmony vocal, guitar; Steve Ledford–fiddle, or (1)unknown lead guitar
Rock Hill, SC, 4 February 1939

| BS 032630-1 | Look On and Cry | Bb B-8120, *County 404 (33)*, *Yazoo 2031 (CD)* |

Clyde Moody–vocal, guitar; Jay Hugh Hall–tenor vocal, guitar; Steve Ledford–fiddle; Wade Mainer–banjo
Rock Hill, SC, 4 February 1939

J.E. MAINER'S MOUNTAINEERS

BS 032635-1	Drunkard's Hiccoughs (1)	Bb B-8400, MW M-7881
BS 032636-1	Country Blues (2)	Bb B-8187, MW M-7881
BS 032637-1	I'm a Poor Pilgrim	MW M-7880
BS 032638-1	Concord Rag (3)	Bb B-8187, MW M-7880

J.E. Mainer–fiddle, (1)vocal; Clyde Moody–guitar, (2)speech; Jay Hugh Hall–
guitar, (1)tenor vocal; (3)Wade Mainer–banjo
Rock Hill, SC, 4 February 1939

WADE MAINER AND SONS OF THE MOUNTAINEERS

BS 041200-1	Sparkling Blue Eyes No. 2	Bb B-8249, MW M-8448

Clyde Moody–vocal, guitar; Jay Hugh Hall–tenor vocal, guitar
Atlanta, 21 August 1939

BS 041201-1	The Poor Drunkard's Dream	Bb B-8273, MW M-8449, *County 404 (33)*
BS 041206-1	Why Not Make Heaven Your Home?	Bb B-8340, MW M-8451

(?)Jay Hugh Hall–vocal, guitar; Clyde Moody–guitar
Atlanta, 21 August 1939

BS 041202-1	Were You There?	Bb B-8273, MW M-8449
BS 041205-1	What a Wonderful Saviour Is He	Bb B-8288, MW M-8450

(?)Jay Hugh Hall–vocal, guitar; Clyde Moody–harmony vocal, guitar; Wade
Mainer–harmony vocal, banjo
Atlanta, 21 August 1939

BS 041203-1	The Gospel Cannon Ball	Bb B-8249, MW M-8448

Wade Mainer–vocal, banjo; Jay Hugh Hall–guitar; Clyde Moody–guitar
Atlanta, 21 August 1939

BS 041204-1	The Great and Final Judgment (1)	Bb B-8288, MW M-8450
BS 041207-1	Mansions In the Sky (1)	Bb B-8340, MW M-8451, *County 404 (33)*
BS 041208-1	Not a Word Of That Be Said (1)	Bb B-8359, MW M-8452, *OH 194 (33), OHCD-4013 (CD)*
BS 041209-1	Drifting Through an Unfriendly World	Bb B-8359, MW M-8452, *OH 194 (33), OHCD-4013 (CD)*

Wade Mainer–vocal, banjo; Clyde Moody–harmony vocal, guitar; Jay Hugh Hall–guitar, (1)tenor vocal
Atlanta, 21 August 1939

The following were made for the Library of Congress Archive of Folk Song by Alan Lomax shortly after the band's command appearance at the White House on 17 February 1941. They were recorded in the form of a simulated broadcast and assigned reference numbers AFS 4490 A1 through B7 on the original 16-inch lacquer disc.

Mountaineers in Asheville (Theme and Introduction)	*OH 124 (33)*
John Henry Was a Little Boy	*OH 124 (33)*
Down In the Willow Garden	*OH 124 (33)*
Sally Goodin	*OH 124 (33)*
Barbara Allen [*Howard Dixon solo*]	*OH 124 (33)*

Cacklin' Pullet	*OH 124 (33)*	
Arkansas Traveler	*OH 124 (33)*	
Sally Ann	*OH 124 (33)*	
Give My Love to Nell	*OH 124 (33)*	
Old Hen She Cackled	*OH 124 (33)*	
Orange Blossom Special	*OH 124 (33)*	
What'cha Gonna Do With a Baby-O	*OH 124 (33)*	
Way Down Yonder In the Cumberland Mountains (Closing theme)	*OH 124 (33)*	

Wade Mainer-–vocal, banjo; Tiny Dodson–vocal, fiddle; Howard Dixon–vocal, steel guitar; Curly Shelton–vocal, mandolin; Jack Shelton–vocal, guitar; Marty Lyles–announcer
WWNC, Asheville, February 1941

BS 071014-1	Shake My Mother's Hand For Me	Bb B-8848
BS 071015-1	Anywhere Is Home	Bb B-8965, *OH OHCD-4013 (CD)*
BS 071016-1	I Can Tell You the Time	Bb B-8965, *OH OHCD-4013 (CD)*
BS 071017-1	He Gave His Life	Bb B-8887, *OH 194 (33)*
BS 071018-1	Ramblin' Boy [*Wade Mainer solo*]	Bb B-8990, *County 404 (33)*
BS 071019-1	The Precious Jewel	Bb B-8887, RCA 20-2159, *County 404 (33)*
BS 071020-1	Old Ruben [*Wade Mainer solo*]	Bb B-8990, *County 404 (33)*, *Rounder CD 1145 (CD)*

BS 071021-1	Precious Memories	Bb B-8848, *OH OHCD-4013 (CD)*

Wade Mainer–vocal, banjo; Curly Shelton–vocal, mandolin; Jack Shelton–vocal, guitar
Atlanta, 29 September 1941

BS 071019 and BS 071021 are duets by the Sheltons with guitar only.

WADE MAINER'S MOUNTAINEERS (or WADE MAINER)

K-2385	Mother's Prayers Have Followed Me	King 603, *769 1023 (33), OH OHCD-4021 (CD)*
K-2386	Vision of Mother (Oscar O. Wilson)	King unissued
	I Saw My Mother Praying	*OH OHCD-4021 (CD)*
K-2387	Don't Write to Mother Too Late (Wade E. Mainer)	King 640, *769 (33), EP478 (45), OH OHCD-4021 (CD)*
	Vision of Mother	King 872
K-2388	I'm Glad I'm On the Inside Looking Out (Wade E. Mainer)	King 872, *769 (33), OH OHCD-4021 (CD)*
K-2389	Awaiting the Return of My Boy	King 640, *OH OHCD-4021 (CD)*
K-2390	Roll My Lady Roll	King unissued
K-2391	There'll Come a Time [*Arville Freeman solo*]	King 603
K-2392	As Time Rolls On [*Arville Freeman solo*]	King unissued

KING RECORDS, 1946

King Records flyer.

WADE One time Syd Nathan from the King Record Company wanted me to come down and do a session for him. When I said I didn't think I could make it, he run his hand down in his pocket and he pulled out a wad of money as big as my fist and said, "I got the money to pay you." A lot of people said he'd beat around the bush, but never me. He always treated me nice. When we got down to Cincinnati, we went to the place where we was to record. It seems like it was an old dry-cleaning joint, big place with plate glass windows in the front. They had all the machines set up to do their recordings. We went down there and Syd Nathan got us all set up.

Syd was the one who pushed me into doing "Dust On the Bible." He said, "I got a telegram from the Bailes Brothers," who wanted him to get me to do it. The Bailes Brothers was going pretty big at that time. I don't think their record of it was on the market yet, and they sent me the words to it. I didn't want to do it at first, but I looked it over and decided it might be pretty good. My band wasn't used to it and we had to rehearse a lot, but we finally got it. Arville Freeman was playing the mandolin for me at that time. He couldn't take the break like I wanted him to and he couldn't kick it off. I didn't want to do the song unless we could do it right. Nathan said he knew someone who'd play the mandolin for me. That was Jethro Burns.

He stepped in while we were recording and said, "They want me to see if I can start this song like you want it done and see if we can put it over." I said, "OK, we'll try it, Jethro. If you can do the parts in the mandolin, we might do a good job." We went over it once or twice and there wasn't a problem. Musicians who know what they're doing can get together and do what they want to anyway. The way I did it was pleasing to them and also to the company, so I guess I done pretty good on it!

I worked on "Searching For a Soldier's Grave" pretty hard too, and I was proud of it. "There'll Come a Time" was an old, old song from way back before my time. I believe Charlie Poole put that out before I did.

I was working for General Motors in 1960 when King Records found out I was here in Flint. They give me a contract and wanted me to do a session for 'em. So I had a couple of boys with me and went down and done some old songs.

K-2393	Dust On the Bible (J. and W. Bailes)*	King 574, 769 (33), 807 (33), EP478 (45), OH OHCD-4021 (CD)
K-2394	Soldier's Grave (J. and W. Bailes)*	King 585, OH OHCD-4021 (CD)
K-2395	Little Pal	King 574, 603
K-2396	He's Coming to Us Dead	King 585, OH OHCD-4021 (CD)

Wade Mainer–vocal, banjo; Oscar (Red) Wilson–tenor vocal, fiddle; Arville Freeman–vocal, mandolin; Ned Smathers–guitar. *Jethro Burns (mandolin) replaces Freeman.
Cincinnati, ca. October 1946

WADE MAINER

K-3192	Now I Lay Me Down To Sleep	King 990, 769 (33), OH OHCD-4021 (CD)
K-3193	No Place To Lay Your Head	King 990, 769 (33), EP478 (45)
	No Place To Lay His Head	OH OHCD-4021 (CD)
K-3194	God's Radio Phone (Wade Mainer)	King 975, AL 1523, OH OHCD-4021 (CD)
K-3195	He's Passing This Way (Wade Mainer)	King 975, AL 1504 (33), OH OHCD-4021 (CD)
K-3196	Those Blue Eyes I Love (Wade Mainer)*	King 955
K-3197	Little Book (Wade Mainer)*	King 955, OH OHCD-4021 (CD)

K-3198	Courtin' In the Rain*	King unissued
K-3199	*unknown title*	King unissued & lost

Wade Mainer–vocal, guitar or *banjo; Willie Carver–tenor vocal, steel guitar;
Wiley Morris–baritone vocal, guitar
Charlotte, 17 March 1951

Original King releases may have appeared on 45 as well as 78 rpm discs.

K-3296	Little Birdie (Wade Mainer)	King 1093
K-3297	The Girl I Left in Sunny Tennessee (Charlie Poole)	King 1093
K-3298	I'm Not Looking Backward (Wade Mainer)	King 1074, *AL 1557*
	How Long Will You Now Last	*OH OHCD-4021 (CD)*
K-3299	Standing Outside (Wade Mainer)	King 1074, 769, *OH OHCD-4021 (CD), Dust-to-Digital 01 (CD)*
K-3300	That Star Belongs to Me (Wade Mainer)	King 1035, *OH OHCD-4021 (CD)*
K-3301	Dreaming Of a Little Cabin (Wade Mainer) (mandolin and 2 guitars only)	King 1035, *OH OHCD-4021 (CD)*

Wade Mainer–vocal, guitar or banjo; Lloyd Burge–tenor vocal, mandolin;
Marion Hall–vocal, guitar; Troy Brammer–banjo, bass
Cincinnati, November 19, 1951

Marion Hall sings lead on K-3297 and K-3301, replacing Wade Mainer. There is
an unknown fiddler on K-3300, and Troy Brammer replaces Mainer on banjo
on at least some titles. Original King releases were published both as 78 and
45 rpm discs.

WADE MAINER AND THE MOUNTAINEERS

| 1711 | Blue Ridge Mountain Blues | Blue Ridge 109 |
| 6121 | Three Nights In a Bar Room | Blue Ridge 109 |

Wade Mainer–vocal, banjo; Jesse (Lost John) Ray–fiddle; unknown–two guitars
(?)North Wilkesboro, NC, 1952

Blue Ridge 109 was the last Wade Mainer release on 78 rpm. All following issues are long-play (33 1/3) discs unless otherwise specified.

WADE MAINER

K-10711	On the Banks Of the Ohio	King 5499 (45)
K-10712	My Home Is Down In Dixie	King 5499 (45)
K-10713	The Little Brown Church	King 769, 965, 1023
K-10714	The New Bright World	King 769
K-10715	The Hill Lone and Gray*	King 769
K-10716	Building On That Rock*	King 769
K-10717	My Soldier Boy (Julie Mainer)*	King 769, 5514 (45), EP478 (45)
K-10718	Streamlined Religion*	King 769, 965
K-10719	He Signed My Pardon*	King 769

K-10720	I'm a Free Little Bird	King 5514 (45)
K-10721	Home In the Rock	King 769
K-10722	Sweet Heaven Was There*	King unissued

Wade Mainer–vocal, banjo; Owen Bloodworth–tenor vocal, guitar; Ed
Bryant–fiddle; Julia Mae Mainer-guitar, *vocal
Cincinnati, April 7, 1961

All King titles above except K 3199 are included in a 2-CD set: *Wade Mainer:
I'm Not Looking Backward*, Gusto GT2-0957-2. 1961 titles were recorded in
stereo; they were issued in mono only on the original 33 and 45 rpm releases
and in stereo on compact disc.

WADE MAINER & THE PLEASANT VALLEY BOYS

| | Take Me In the Lifeboat* (F. Southern) | Knob KS 202 (45), *OH OHCD-4021 (CD)* |
| | Voice Of My Savior (J. Martin) | Knob KS 202 (45), *OH OHCD-4021 (CD)* |

Wade Mainer–banjo, *vocal, with mandolin, guitar, bass, and harmony
singers
Michigan, 1969

WADE MAINER AND THE SONS OF THE MOUNTAINEERS BACKED UP BY THE STRAITWAY TRIO

	Home In the Rock (W. Mainer)	IRMA ILP 105, OH 90014, *OH OHCD-90014 (CD)*
	Diamonds In the Rough (arr. W. Mainer)	IRMA ILP 105, OH 90014, *OH OHCD-90014 (CD)*
	Hide Me Rock Of Ages (B.C. George)	IRMA ILP 105, OH 90014, *OH OHCD-90014 (CD)*

Great Caravan	IRMA ILP 105, OH 90014, *OH OHCD-90014 (CD)*
Walking the Sea (arr. W. Mainer)	IRMA ILP 105, OH 90014, *OH OHCD-90014 (CD)*
Scarlet Purple Robe (Cowboy Copas)	IRMA ILP 105, OH 90014, *OH OHCD-90014 (CD)*
Gate Is Straight (W. Mainer)	IRMA ILP 105, OH 90014, *OH OHCD-90014 (CD)*
Keep Walking (Tuck)	IRMA ILP 105, OH 90014, *OH OHCD-90014 (CD)*
My Home Sweet Home (Solon Maynord)	IRMA ILP 105, OH 90014, *OH OHCD-90014 (CD)*
Waiting (instrumental) (W. Mainer)	IRMA ILP 105, OH 90014, *OH OHCD-90014 (CD)*
Mainer's Melody (arr. W. Mainer)	IRMA ILP 105, OH 90014, *OH OHCD-90014 (CD)*
Home In the Solid Rock (Solon Maynord)	IRMA ILP 105, OH 90014, *OH OHCD-90014 (CD)*
I'll Live Again (Julia Mainer–Joe Allan)	IRMA ILP 105, OH 90014, *OH OHCD-90014 (CD)*
When I Reach Home (W. Mainer–Joe Allan)	IRMA ILP 105, OH 90014, *OH OHCD-90014 (CD)*

Wade Mainer–vocal, banjo; Straitway Trio (Rev. Charles Cooper, Rodger Cooper, Jim Maynard, Bill Carpenter)–fiddle, banjo, guitar, bass, and vocals, Tommy Crank–producer
Carpenter's Studio, Brighton, MI, late 1960s

IRMA is an abbreviation of International Rural Music of America, Inc. in Jackson, Michigan.

WADE MAINER

Little Log Cabin in the Lane	OH 90168
Who's Been Here Since I've Been Gone	OH 90168
Hard Rocking Chair	OH 90168, OHCD-4000 (CD)
Darby's Ram	OH 90168
Big Eyed Rabbit	OH 90168
Jimmy Brown	OH 90168
An Old Account Was Settled	OH 90168
Mama, You're Awful Mean to Me	OH 90168
Gonna Bring My Baby Back	OH 90168
Little Birdie	OH 90168
Blue Mountain Bells	OH 90168
Wade's Laughing Song	OH 90168
Rovin' Gambler	OH 90168
Trail to Mexico	OH 90168
City on the Hill	OH 90168, OHCD-4000 (CD)
Peg and Awl	OH 90168

Wade Mainer–vocal, banjo; Julia Mae Mainer–vocal, guitar; Virgil Shouse–
bass; Jim Childress–bass, harmony vocal; Roy Cobb–guitar, harmony vocal;
John Morris–bass vocal ("City on the Hill"), Randall J. Mainer–vocal ("An Old
Account Was Settled," "Rovin' Gambler")
Brighton, Michigan(?), ca. 1984

WADE & JULIA MAINER

Ramshackle Shack	June Appal JA 0065D
Be Kind To a Man When He's Down (Fiddling John Carson)	June Appal JA 0065D
Bring Back My Mountain Boy To Me (arr. Mainer)	June Appal JA 0065D
Hobo's Waltz (Wade Mainer)	June Appal JA 0065D
Royal Telephone	June Appal JA 0065D
Charles Lawson (Walter "Kid" Smith)	June Appal JA 0065D
Trickling Water	June Appal JA 0065D
The Land I Love (Away Down Yonder) (arr. Mainer)	June Appal JA 0065D
Down By the Railroad Tracks (Crumit–Curtis)	June Appal JA 0065D
Sugar In the Gourd	June Appal JA 0065D
Down At the End of Memory's Lane (Wade Mainer–Zeke Morris)	June Appal JA 0065D
How Sweet To Walk (Hand In Hand With Jesus) (Wade Mainer)	June Appal JA 0065D
You Will Never Miss Your Mother Until She's Gone (Asher–Sizemore)	June Appal JA 0065D
Cider Mill	June Appal JA 0065D

The Girl I Left In Sunny Tennessee (Braisted–Carter)	June Appal JA 0065D

Wade Mainer–vocal, banjo; Julia Mae Mainer–vocal, guitar; Mel Hammon–fiddle, vocal; Ronald Hammon–guitar
Maggard Sound, Big Stone Gap, VA, 14–16 March, 1991

Peg and Awl*	June Appal JA 0065D
Jonah (arr. Mainer)	June Appal JA 0065D
When It's Time For the Whippoorwill To Sing (Dixon–Stewart)	June Appal JA 0065D
I Can't Sit Down (arr. Mainer)	June Appal JA 0065D

Wade Mainer–vocal, banjo, *harmonica; Julia Mae Mainer–vocal, guitar; Mel Hammon–fiddle, vocal; Ronald Hammon–guitar
Seedtime On the Cumberland Festival, Whitesburg, KY, 31 May 1991

June Appal JA 0065D is a compact disc.

After Wade's retirement from General Motors in 1972, he and Julia resumed performing and recorded LP discs over the next two decades for John Morris's Old Homestead label in Brighton, Michigan. Mr. Morris has provided album titles and numbers of his releases; some have been duplicated on tape cassettes and compact discs. Some sets duplicate previously issued material from Old Homestead and other sources.

Family Album	OH 70034
Old Time Sacred Songs	OH 70065
I Can't Sit Down	OH 70068
How Sweet To Walk	OH 70082
Sacred Songs of Mother and Home	OH OHCS 135, 90001

First Time In Stereo	OH 90002
Mountain Sacred Songs	OH 90016
Old Time Songs	OH 90123
String Band Music	OH 90197
Carolina Mule	OH 90207
From the Maple On the Hill (selections from LP discs)	OH 4000 (CD)
Live for Collectors	OH 4032 (CD)
Original Mountaineers, Volume 1	OH 4043 (CD)
Original Mountaineers, Volume 2	OH 4044 (CD)

Index

Page numbers in **bold** indicate illustrations.